The General Instruction of the Roman Missal, 1969–2002

A Commentary

Dennis C. Smolarski, S.J.

THE LITURGICAL PRESS

Collegeville, Minnesota

www.litpress.org

N.B. When this book was released by The Liturgical Press to its printer in early March 2003, an officially approved English translation of the 2002 version of the General Instruction of the Roman Missal for the United States was not available. In the hope of helping Roman Catholics to understand the changes, which in some dioceses were implemented in Advent 2002, The Liturgical Press has made this book available as quickly as possible. Translations were based on the 1982 published text of the General Instruction.

Cover design by Ann Blattner

1   2   3   4   5   6   7   8

Library of Congress Cataloging-in-Publication Data

Smolarski, Dennis Chester, 1947–
    The general instruction of the Roman Missal, 1969–2002:
a commentary / Dennis C. Smolarski.
        p.   cm.
    Includes bibliographical references.
    ISBN 0-8146-2936-9
    1. Catholic Church. General instruction of the Roman missal.   I. Title.

BX2015.S66   2003
264'.023—dc21   2003044682

Contents

Preface

The "What" and the "Why"

Much of human experience is often subdivided into two categories, one pertaining to activity and what can be perceived by the senses, and the other pertaining to reflection and things unseen. Spiritual writers sometimes make the distinction between *contemplation* and *action,* and philosophers sometimes distinguish between *theory* and *practice.*[1] Another way of making the distinction is to speak about the *what* in contrast to the *why.*

Much of our Catholic liturgical life is concerned with visible actions, sensible objects, and audible words—the "matter and form" of the sacraments and the core of other liturgical and devotional activities. And it is proper to be concerned about what we see and hear. But sometimes it is also helpful to understand what lies beneath the actions, namely the *theory,* the *why.* To be able to experience more fully the graces that result from our liturgical activity and even from what we do in our day-to-day lives, it helps if we stop, *reflect* on our actions, and at times even *contemplate* God's influence in what has occurred.

It is so easy to focus on the *what.* In the late 1960s and early 1970s, Catholics learned a lot about *what* to do in the revised Mass. Unfortunately, not too many people were told *why.* We focused on the *practice,* but often neglected the *theory.* Certainly it is necessary to pay attention to revised rubrics, but often the individual rubrics (and rubrical changes) only make sense when one sees them from the vantage point of reflecting on the whole and, out of this reflection, comes to understand the *why.*

In March 2002, the third edition of the Roman Missal was published in Latin, including a revised version of the General Instruction of the Roman Missal (2002 GIRM) of which a preliminary version had been made public in July 2000. It is tempting to want to focus on the *what* of the relatively few major rubrical changes or textual additions in the 2002 GIRM and neglect the bigger picture. Those interested in the details of the changes might want to skip immediately to chapter 4, and then read chapter 6 and the appendix, and only later page through the other sections.

But it is my hope that this moment in the history of the liturgy will provide Western Catholics an opportunity (and perhaps a desire) to *reflect* on the *why* of the liturgy, a reflection that was done relatively briefly and somewhat superficially thirty years ago when the revised Roman Missal, approved by Pope Paul VI in 1970, was published and began to shape the regular form of worship used by Catholics of the Roman Rite. Over forty years have passed since the Second Vatican Council was formally opened, and we have learned much about the Church, about liturgy, about our world in that time. We have struggled to implement the "new Mass" and, in general, have made great strides in the way we worship. Perhaps the 2002 publication of the third edition of the Roman Missal that was revised at the request of Vatican II, and its implementation in parishes and schools will lead us further along the path toward that "full, conscious, and active participation" desired by the council fathers (see the Constitution on the Sacred Liturgy, no. 14).

Reflection on the *why,* however, should lead readers to review the history of changes in the Mass and also reflect on some of the more important *non-rubrical* themes that surface in the latest revision of the Roman Missal. This history and these non-rubrical themes are the reasons for including the historical background in the first few chapters and the analysis given in chapter 7.

The Context: A Text in Flux and Subject to Modification

A few additional preliminary comments may be helpful to understand the context for examining the latest revision of a document that so intimately affects the worship of our God by Western Catholics.

Between the initial version of the GIRM, which appeared in late 1969, and the publication of the complete Roman Missal revised after Vatican II, which appeared less than a year later in early 1970, changes were introduced into the GIRM, some of which will be noted later. Something similar happened between July 2000, when a preliminary version of the revised GIRM was made public, and March 2002, when the third edition of the Roman Missal appeared. The Latin text of the 2000 GIRM contained misspellings, incorrect footnotes, inconsistencies, and erroneous cross-references. Most of these were corrected when the third edition of the Latin Roman Missal was published in March 2002, yet a few other changes were introduced as well. At minimum, such facts tell us that the GIRM is a living, changing document, unlike its Tridentine predecessors.

Furthermore, the norms contained in the 2002 GIRM are subject to further specifications by national conferences of bishops.[2] Permission may even be granted to modify certain of these general norms (as the United States bishops did in 1970 regarding the use of white vestments at funerals or regarding the practice of kneeling after the *Sanctus* until the final doxology of the eucharistic prayer). Although it is important to understand the principles found in the 2002 GIRM (since the GIRM governs the celebration of the Roman Mass throughout the world), it is also important to know the specifications and additional adaptations approved by national conferences of bishops. In the United States, such clarifications, in the past, were included in an appendix to the GIRM found with all the Roman documents at the beginning of the Sacramentary. In the future, any specifications or modifications of the norms of the General Instruction will be incorporated into the actual text of the GIRM. In addition, a collection of guidelines and specific rules, entitled *Norms for the Celebration and Reception of Holy Communion Under Both Kinds in the Dioceses of the United States of America,* was approved by the United States bishops in June 2001 as a revision of the earlier 1984 document *This Holy and Living Sacrifice* and subsequently confirmed by the Vatican in

March 2002. These norms also should be read in conjunction with the 2002 GIRM.

It may be some time until official translations of the 2002 GIRM become readily available in the various languages in which Mass is celebrated in North America and such translations approved and modified by the various national conferences of bishops—and subsequently recognized by Rome. Until that time, one may want to review the 1975 GIRM (with the slight modifications introduced by the 1983 Code of Canon Law), the latest text of the GIRM commonly found in current editions of the English Sacramentary or vernacular editions of the Roman Missal in other languages. Since much of the text and the underlying principles have *not* changed, a review of the guidelines in the earlier versions of the GIRM, guidelines that shape our celebrations of the Eucharist, may provide a good foundation for an in-depth study of the 2002 GIRM in the months and years ahead. Such a review should provide a foundation for an ongoing reflection on how we celebrate Christ's death and resurrection whenever we gather around the Lord's table.

In what follows, the reader may feel overwhelmed by numerous cross-references to various versions of the GIRM. Since this book is intended as an introduction to and overview of the 2002 GIRM and of the Order of Mass in the 2002 Missal, such references are necessary for anyone who wants to read the primary text and compare it to previous versions. The task is made more complicated since the 2002 GIRM (and its preliminary version, the 2000 GIRM) has *renumbered* the paragraphs of previous versions, while keeping most of the original divisions into chapters and subsections. Readers should assume that references are to the 2002 GIRM, unless specifically noted otherwise. To assist in identifying references, however, where the 2002 GIRM substantially agrees with the 1975 GIRM, the older number is added with a subscript in square brackets, e.g., 2002 GIRM 69 [45_{1975}]. Where the discussion focuses on the older versions of the GIRM, a reference to the 2002 GIRM is included in brackets. As will be noted in chapter 3, various versions of the GIRM preceded the 2000 and 2002 documents, but since all these earlier versions use essentially the same numbering for paragraphs, the references to any early version will usually be to the commonly-available 1975 text.

This book grew out of a presentation on the revised GIRM given to the clergy and pastoral ministers of the Diocese of San José, California. My thanks to Bishop Patrick J. McGrath and the San José diocesan office of liturgy for inviting me to address the liturgical leaders of that diocese. Special thanks are also due to others who have read various drafts of the written texts, in particular Msgr. Joseph M. Champlin; Sr. Agnes Cunningham, S.S.C.M.; Fr. J. Michael Joncas; Msgr. Frederick R. McManus; Sr. Mary Alice Piil, C.S.J.; Fr. George F. Remm; and others.

May the Lord help us on our pilgrim journey toward the new and eternal Jerusalem, especially as we stop along the way to celebrate who we are as priestly people, ever nourished at the table of God's Word and of Christ's Body and Blood.

Notes

[1] See Boethius, *Contemplation of Philosophy,* Book I, prose 1, where the initial letters of *theory* and *practice* are embroidered on the gown of Lady Philosophy.

[2] Early in the previous GIRM (no. 6), there was a strong statement about each conference of bishops having the power to enact norms suited to local traditions and the character of the people. This general permission has now been replaced by a new chapter 9 on adaptations that conferences of bishops can make which also includes the procedures that need to be followed.

CHAPTER 1

Past, Present, Future

In the First Letter to the Corinthians, Saint Paul writes, "everything must be done properly and in order" (14:40). The natural human tendency to try to put order into chaos and to create social rituals to help guide human behavior is reflected in the Church's practice of organizing its common worship according to established traditions. The nature of human ritual demands repetition, and repetition requires organized patterns of behavior. Such patterns of behavior, which occur in various aspects of human life, provide the basis, after theological reflection, for the liturgical laws and rubrics that guide and direct public worship in many Christian communities.

When reflecting on history, human beings typically subdivide their experience into *past, present,* and *future.* In liturgy, as in other aspects of life, people have found it helpful to use these common historical categories. During the great eucharistic prayer, we often acclaim the mystery of our faith using such categories. We remember the past, that *Christ has died.* We affirm a present reality, that *Christ is risen.* We proclaim our future hope, that *Christ will come again.*[1] These same categories have been and continue to be used to aid our individual and communal spiritual growth. For example, Saint Ignatius of Loyola, in his manual for retreats, the *Spiritual Exercises,* proposed a meditation at the end of which retreatants ponder a crucifix and ask themselves questions

1

related to *past, present,* and *future,* "What have I done for Christ? What am I doing for Christ? What should I do for Christ?" (cf. *Spiritual Exercises,* no. 53).

There are many other opportunities for similar types of self-reflection. In fact, any significant moment in a person's history as well as in the history of the Church's liturgy can be an opportunity for people to reflect on similar questions, such as, What has been done? What is being done? What should be done? It is most appropriate to ponder these questions as we reflect on the public, communal worship of our God, through Christ, guided by the Spirit. The publication of the third edition of the Roman Missal in March 2002 with an updated version of the General Instruction of the Roman Missal (GIRM) provides us with a privileged moment to reflect on the liturgy in terms of *past, present,* and *future.*

The GIRM was initially published in 1969 as part of the revision of the Mass mandated by Vatican II. The latest revision gives us the opportunity to reflect on the liturgical principles highlighted for us by the Second Vatican Council as well as on the revised rite of the Mass that has been in common use since 1970. In fact, the publication of the third edition of the Missal and of the 2002 GIRM challenges us to review our practices to see how well the liturgical experiences in our churches and chapels live up to the ideal presented by all the liturgical documents published since the council. It is so easy to fall into habits, good or bad, and forget about *why* we do *what* we do, and so it can be very good for us to take the opportunity to stop and reflect.

The Catholic liturgical tradition is a sacramental tradition, one in which public worship and the use of elements of God's creation, such as water, oil, bread, and wine, play significant roles. The ancient maxim *lex orandi, lex credendi,* emphasizing the connection between the *rule of prayer* and the *rule of faith* (Intro. GIRM 2), explains why liturgical services have always played both formative and expressive roles in the faith life of Catholics.[2] The connection between faith and worship is also one reason why changes in the way in which Catholics worship can elicit strong reactions—because some may interpret *changes in external rituals* as reflective of some sort of *modifications of eternal truths*. This link partially explains the resistance that appeared in the late 1960s and early 1970s when the Mass began to be celebrated in local languages and when the revised Order of Mass was promulgated.

It is also important to remember that no document or rite is perfect. Because documents, even ecclesiastical documents, are created by fallible and sinful human beings, they will always be less than ideal and will usually have come about as a result of a compromise between vision and inertia. There is a Swedish proverb that goes: "Break your chains and you are free; cut your roots and you die." The challenge with growth, in liturgy as in life, is to determine what are our *roots* that keep us solidly grounded and faithful to what is important in our history, and what are the *chains* that keep us enslaved. Unfortunately, the distinction between *roots* and *chains* is rarely crystal clear. This is one reason why liturgical change seems so painfully slow to some of the faithful and irreverently fast to others. Even the far-reaching Constitution on the Sacred Liturgy (CSL), *Sacrosanctum Concilium,* of the Second Vatican Council was a product of compromises, and it juxtaposes visionary principles with what may seem today to be odd restrictions. Fortunately, CSL provided a breadth of openness to development of the widest kind (especially in nos. 4 and 37–40), going far beyond the uses of the Roman Rite (nos. 4, 40).

Given these caveats, we can use the publication of the third edition of the Roman Missal with the revised 2002 GIRM as an occasion for a continued renewal of the liturgy, the "source and summit" of the Church's activity (CSL 10). Thus, rather than becoming narrowly focused on minute rubrical changes, we should use this moment to reflect on the bigger picture that every version of the GIRM has called the Church to see.

To begin this reflection, let us first recall briefly some history related to the Roman Missal.

Notes

[1] The Latin acclamation is in the form of a prayer to Christ: "We announce your death, O Lord, and we confess your resurrection, until you come," but also highlights the *past* (death), *present* (resurrection), and *future* (return). The common English version, a free rendering of the Latin original by the International Commission on English in the Liturgy (ICEL), is in the form of a proclamatory acclamation in the style of Psalm 117, for example, and the equivalent has also been included in the Polish translation of the Roman Missal (as acclamation four).

[2] The original text, *"legem credendi lex statuat supplicandi,"* is attributed to the fifth-century writer Prosper of Acquitaine (see *Catechism of the Catholic Church,* no. 1124). Historically, it has been used as a maxim that justifies appealing to the prayer tradition of the Church to justify doctrinal positions. For example, see *Munificentissimus Deus* of Pius XII (1 November 1950), in which the Pope appeals to the liturgical traditions of East and West (in nos. 16–18) in forming a basis for the declaration of the assumption of Mary.

CHAPTER 2

History
What has been done?

The 1970 revised Roman Missal promulgated by Pope Paul VI, as well as the revised 2002 third edition of the Roman Missal with the 2002 GIRM published with the approval of Pope John Paul II, did not appear out of nowhere. These missals are in continuity with the tradition found in the liturgical books of the Roman Church, a tradition that has existed for at least a thousand years. In addition, these missals immediately follow upon the missal published in 1570 after the Council of Trent. Before looking at the 2002 Roman Missal, let us briefly recall some liturgical history for, as the American philosopher George Santayana has wisely said, "Those who cannot remember the past are condemned to repeat it."

The 1570 Roman Missal

The evolution of the eucharistic liturgy in the Western Church has a long and complicated history. Prior to the 1500s, much variation existed from area to area in the celebration of the Mass. It was the Council of Trent, in the late sixteenth century, that attempted to impose some uniformity in liturgical practices. The council recognized the benefits of some sort of liturgical reform, but did not provide any visionary document to guide such a reform. As the council closed, it handed over the revision of the liturgical books to the Roman See. In a sense, Trent's approach to liturgical reform could be considered "modern" in that it entrusted the task of reform to a group of professional scholars and it made use of the relatively new invention of the printing press to disseminate the revised liturgical books far and wide. Nevertheless, certain areas or groups that had their own traditions and practices continued to observe them even after the reforms of Trent. For example, Milan used its own Ambrosian Rite, Toledo used the Mozarabic Rite, and the Dominicans and Carmelites had special traditions within the Roman Rite.

The Roman Missal, revised at the direction of the Council of Trent and published in 1570, included the form of celebrating Mass that was common in Rome. Pope Saint Pius V, in the Apostolic Constitution *Quo Primum* (14 July 1570) which promulgated the 1570 Missal, declared the "restoration" of the Missal to be "*ad pristinam . . . sanctorum Patrum normam* (according to the ancient . . . norm of the holy Fathers)." Unfortunately, historical and liturgical scholarship in the sixteenth century was not what it is now, and many historical documents had not yet been discovered or critically analyzed. Thus the task of "restoration" was less than ideal. In fact, the Introduction to the GIRM of the 1970 Missal states that the 1570 Missal differed very little from the first printed edition of the Missal, which appeared in 1474, and that edition in turn followed the Missal used at the time of Pope Innocent III who died in 1216 (Intro. GIRM 7).

Using the manuscripts available to them, the scholars entrusted by Trent with revising the Missal set about their task, and in 1570 a new standardized Roman Missal was compiled, published, and promulgated as binding on the majority of Western Catholics. To provide norms for the celebration of Mass, the Missal included three introductory sections that appeared before the liturgical texts themselves, and these three sections focused on the ritual and rubrical elements of the Mass. One additional document explained the liturgical year, the liturgical seasons, and the calendar.

The first of the introductory sections was entitled *Rubricae Generales Missalis* (General Rubrics of the Missal). It included an overview of the Order of Mass as well as general norms about the ranks of feasts, the choice of Mass texts, the time for celebrating Mass, the color of vestments, the preparation of the altar, and other related topics.

The second section was entitled *Ritus Servandus in Celebratione Missae* (The Rite to be Observed in the Celebration of Mass). This section gave detailed instructions for the priest and the server about how to celebrate Mass. These instructions found their historical origin in the Roman *Ordines,* booklets of rubrics for Masses celebrated by the pope that date to around the seventh century. The rubrical instructions that appeared in the 1570 Missal were based on a work compiled by the papal master of ceremonies, John Burchard of Strassburg, which appeared in 1502, but reworked so that the basic texts described what may be called a "private Mass."[1]

The 1570 *Ritus Servandus* reflected the manner in which Mass was celebrated in the sixteenth century, a time in which the people received communion infrequently (and never from the chalice) and in which the majority of people did not understand the Latin language used at Mass. Although instructions were included in the *Ritus Servandus* for the deacon and subdeacon regarding their ministry at a "Solemn Mass," notably absent were references to the participation of the assembly. In fact, even the description about the Communion of the people during Mass seemed to be an afterthought (cf. *Ritus Servandus,* Pt. 10, no. 6, *Si qui sunt communicandi in Missa* [If anyone is to receive Communion at Mass], no. 9, *Si in Missa solemni fiat Communio,* [If Communion occurs at a solemn Mass]).

Following the *Ritus Servandus* was a third section entitled *De Defectibus in Celebratione Missarum Occurrentibus* (Concerning Defects Occurring in the Celebration of Masses). This section enumerated the various types of problems that could occur during Mass and what should be done if they actually did occur. For example, it included instructions on what a priest should do if he discovered that water rather than wine had been poured into the chalice.

The text of these three introductory rubrical sections did not change substantially in the almost 400 years between 1570 and the 1950s at which time the rites of Holy Week were revised by Pope Pius XII.[2] A major revision of the first section, the *Rubricae Generales,* did not occur until 1960 and of the second section, the *Ritus Servandus,* not until 1965. These three initial sections focused on rules and on the actions of the clergy and assisting ministers, and priests were taught to follow the rubrics exactly. Some priests even developed scruples because of worrying about forgetting one or the other rubric. The focus on the rubrics and on following them exactly was reflected in other texts also found in the Missal. For example, one of the prayers found in more recent printings of the 1570 Missal and appointed to be said as part of the thanksgiving after Mass was the prayer, *Obsecro te, dulcissime Domine Iesu Christe* (I beseech you, most sweet Lord Jesus Christ). It included an introductory note: "To the one who recites the following prayer on bended knees (unless impeded), there is conceded the remission of defects and faults committed through human frailty in the celebration of Mass."

The 1969 Order of Mass

In approving the Constitution on the Sacred Liturgy on 4 December 1963, the Second Vatican Council ordered a revision of the Mass (CSL 50–58). It decreed that the "the rite of the Mass is to be revised in such a way that the intrinsic nature and purpose of its several parts, as also the connection between them, can be more clearly manifested, and that devout and active participation by the faithful can be more easily accomplished" (CSL 50). This decree shifted the focus during the celebration of liturgy to awareness by the faithful rather than "mere observance" of the rubrics (CSL 11) and to "full, conscious, and active participation" by the faithful (CSL 14). The revision of the liturgical rites was entrusted to the Consilium, a special Vatican commission of bishops and liturgical scholars, established by Pope Paul VI in January 1964, who consulted widely as they went about their task. After several years of careful work by the Consilium, the revised Order of Mass was approved by Pope Paul VI on 3 April 1969 and the text of the revised Mass was published along with the General Instruction of the Roman Missal on 18 November 1969.[3]

The Order of Mass made public in 1969 was not so much a new creation but rather an evolution in the rite of the Mass of the Roman Rite. The basic structure of the Mass was kept intact but changes were introduced based on a renewed understanding of the origins and the purpose of various sections of the liturgy. There were also some compromises, such as the introduction of a *communal, public* act of penitence paralleling the *ministerial, semiprivate* prayers said at the foot of the altar in the 1570 Missal. In responding to the wishes of the Vatican Council, overall the revision helped clarify the purposes and interconnections of the various parts of the Mass.

Above all, the Mass was revised with the participation of the people in mind, and the directions found in the GIRM repeatedly make reference to the people and their participation. The opening paragraph of the 1969 GIRM, retained in the 2002 GIRM (2002 GIRM 16 [1_{1975}])[4] with only the addition of the words "in the Holy Spirit," proclaims that the celebration of the Mass is "the action of Christ and the people of God." Two paragraphs later (2002 GIRM 18 [3_{1975}]) we read, "The Church desires this kind of participation, the nature of the celebration demands it, and for the Christian people it is a right and duty they have by reason of their baptism." The presence and participation of God's holy people in the celebration of the Mass was a presupposition in the 1969 Order of Mass and in the completely revised Roman Missal that first appeared in 1970. Other details flowed from this basic principle. For example, reorienting the position of the priest at the altar to face the assembly, following the practice of the ancient Roman basilicas, was merely one sign of this concern about the people present during the celebration of the Eucharist.[5] (Such attention to the people is also found in other liturgical books and documents such as the General Introduction to Christian Initiation, no. 7, and the introduction to the *Book of Blessings,* no. 16.)

To many people, the Mass in the 1570 Missal seemed to be merely a series of disconnected rites, the majority of which were performed with the priest at the altar. Taken together, they seemed to lack any interrelationships. The 1570 Missal also betrayed an unfortunate clericalization of the liturgy, in that the presiding priest himself had to recite all the texts, even though certain texts may also have been said or sung by someone else (e.g., the presiding priest had to recite the *Introit* even though the choir sang it, and had to read the scriptural texts, even though they were also proclaimed by the subdeacon and deacon). The origin of some practices was unknown to the compilers of the 1570 Missal, but more recent research into liturgical history gave us insights into the origin and purpose of the various actions and, in some cases, pastoral sensitivity suggested a revision that responded to contemporary needs. As a result, the 1969 Order of Mass, though based on the 1570 Order of Mass, was imbued with a new spirit and vision.

There are several levels on which the older Missal and Order of Mass were revised to produce the 1969 Order of Mass and the GIRM. There were, of course, revisions in the actual texts and in some of the liturgical rites. The presiding priest was also given options among various prayer texts (e.g., the forms of the act of penitence) and the liberty to speak to the assembly in his own words (e.g., the initial introduction). In addition, the 1969 Order of Mass also addressed the issue of liturgical *place*. No longer was it supposed that the entire liturgy took place at the altar (or at the foot of the altar). The 1969 GIRM reintroduced the vision of the early Church, that the liturgy takes place primarily where the people of God are gathered and participate in a communal activity (2002 GIRM 288 [253$_{1975}$], 294 [257$_{1975}$]). At certain moments, the attention of the assembly is focused on one of several different locations within the larger liturgical space (most often at one of the key locations in the sanctuary, but sometimes at the font in the baptistery, or even at the door of the church). Each church should have a *sanctuary* wherein are located the chair for the presiding priest, the altar, and the ambo (2002 GIRM 295), but the liturgy does not occur exclusively at any one of these locations.

Thus, in the 1969 GIRM, there was a return to an older tradition of reserving the ambo for the proclamation of the readings during the Liturgy of the Word, of using the presidential chair (or bishop's *cathedra*) for leading prayer during the introductory and concluding rites, and of focusing on the altar only when the bread and the wine are there during the Liturgy of the Eucharist and the eucharistic action is taking place. The use of varied locations, in fact, derives from the nature of the liturgical action and better helps the assembly focus on certain aspects of the mystery being celebrated during the liturgy.

Structurally then, the 1969 Order of Mass has four major sections.

1. The Introductory Rites

After the people have gathered, the celebration typically begins with those assembled joining in song to express their unity (2002 GIRM 47 [25$_{1975}$]). This action of singing is usually the first part of the opening rites and a key moment that helps transform a group of disparate individuals into the gathered body of Christ. The introductory rites also usually include the entrance procession, the veneration and optional incensation of the altar, an initial formal greeting between the presiding priest and the rest of the assembly, an act of penitence or the sprinkling with blessed water, and on some days the *Gloria,* and they always conclude with the first major presidential prayer, the collect or opening prayer.

After the procession and the veneration (and incensation) of the altar, the presiding priest goes to the presidential chair at which he ideally remains until the end of the Liturgy of the Word and from which he leads this introductory section of the Mass.[6] On special occasions, for example on Palm Sunday, or when Morning Prayer or Evening Prayer is joined to Mass, or at the ordination of a bishop, some introductory elements may be changed, but this section always includes some sort of procession to the sanctuary and concludes with the collect.

In the 1570 Missal, the penitential element was a private dialogue between the priest and the server done at the "foot of the altar," that is, standing before the steps leading up to the altar. At a solemn or a high Mass, this penitential dialogue took place while the choir was finishing the singing of the *Introit* (entrance chant) and was inaudible to others present. Also in the 1570 Missal, the blessing and sprinkling of holy water was an optional, auxiliary rite done prior to the major Mass on Sundays, but not really part of it. The other components prior to the collect and the readings were all done with the priest at the altar. In addition, to some the order of elements seemed strange, for example, including the incensation between the *Confiteor* and the *Kyrie*.

The 1969 Order of Mass retained the primary elements of the introductory rites of the 1570 Mass, yet arranged them into a more or less coherent opening section to help prepare those assembled to hear God's Word and celebrate Christ's eucharistic banquet.

2. The Liturgy of the Word

After coming together as one family in Christ and acknowledging its need for God's merciful love, the assembly now shifts its focus to a different part of the church—the ambo, the "table" of God's Word (2002 GIRM 28 [8_{1975}]). Readers and the deacon proclaim the readings there, and it is from there that the psalmist or cantor leads the responsorial psalm.

The post-Vatican II reform introduced the practice of proclaiming three readings at Masses on Sundays and major feasts. It also revised the scriptural response to the first reading to take the form of the responsorial psalm. This psalm, in reality, is a proclamation of Scripture in its own right that is normally sung and involves the participation of the entire assembly by means of the refrain. In addition, the *Alleluia* (or Lenten replacement) is now construed as a preparation for the gospel rather than a response to the previous reading. It is to be sung, with everyone standing, during the procession with the Book of the Gospels to the ambo.

After the readings, the homily, and the Creed (when used), the Liturgy of the Word concludes with the restored prayer of the faithful or general intercessions in which the assembly fulfills its baptismal duty to intercede for the needs of the Church and the world.

3. The Liturgy of the Eucharist

After the assembly has been nourished at the table of God's Word, its focus shifts to the altar, the "table . . . of Christ's Body" (2002 GIRM 28 [8₁₉₇₅]). The priest, accompanied by the deacon, moves from the chair to the altar, returning to the chair after the Communion of the assembly. The altar is prepared and the offerings of bread and wine may be brought up in procession by members of the assembly and given to the priest and deacon, who then formally place them on the altar. The 1969 Order of Mass clarifies the purpose and meaning of this section of the liturgical celebration. Its structure is now more clearly based on the biblical institution narratives that highlight the four verbs: *take, bless, break,* and *give* (2002 GIRM 72 [48₁₉₇₅]).

What occurs at the altar prior to the eucharistic prayer corresponds to the action of *taking.* It is now seen, therefore, as a preparation rite, and *not* (as was often taught in catechetical materials prior to Vatican II) as an "offertory" (which, in fact, occurs within the eucharistic prayer immediately after the institution narrative, see 2002 GIRM 79f [55f₁₉₇₅]). The prayers during this preparation rite have been simplified from those contained in the 1570 Missal and they accompany the placement of the elements of bread and wine on the altar after these offerings are received from the people. This preparation of the gifts concludes with the prayer over the offerings, now said aloud rather than privately, as in the 1570 Missal.

The biblical action of *blessing* corresponds to the great eucharistic prayer. The single eucharistic prayer in the 1570 Missal, known as the Roman Canon, was augmented by three other prayers, one based on a text found in the *Apostolic Tradition* attributed to Hippolytus of Rome, commonly dated to around the year 215, and another based on a version of the Anaphora of Saint Basil, used widely in Eastern Churches. Subsequently, eucharistic prayers for Masses of Reconciliation, for Masses with Children, and for Masses for Various Needs and Occasions were approved for use and now all appear in the third edition of the Missal.

After the eucharistic prayer, the assembly prepares itself for the *breaking* of the bread and the reception of the *gift* that is

Communion. The Our Father is now a communal prayer rather than being recited by the priest alone, as in the 1570 Missal.[7] The sign of peace is once again restored to the assembly as a whole and the breaking of the bread is simplified to a form it had in earlier centuries. Communion may be given to all under both kinds in situations enumerated in the GIRM (2002 GIRM 283 [242₁₉₇₅]). After a period of silence, with the priest normally seated at the presidential chair, this section of the Mass is concluded with the prayer after Communion.

4. The Concluding Rites

Now that the Liturgy of the Eucharist has been concluded, the assembly's focus once again returns to the presidential chair. Normally the priest remains at the chair and from there he leads the brief concluding section of the Mass. The concluding rites consist merely of brief announcements (if necessary), a greeting, a blessing, and the dismissal by the deacon. If, however, another liturgical action immediately follows the Eucharist, for example, the final commendation at a funeral Mass, the typical concluding rites are omitted.

The 1969 General Instruction of the Roman Missal

The 1969 GIRM covered, in an abbreviated manner, the details of the earlier *Rubricae Generales, Ritus Servandus,* and *De Defectibus,* but, unlike the earlier documents, the 1969 GIRM also provided a theological overview of what was happening during the celebration of the Mass. In particular, it included pastoral explanations of the meaning of the various parts of the Mass, explanations based on solid historical research and liturgical principles, rather than on pious allegorical images such as were commonly found in prayer books and various catechisms prior to the Second Vatican Council. The 1969 GIRM consisted of 341 numbered sections divided into eight chapters. These chapters have remained the same through the various revisions of the GIRM, including the most recent. The chapters of the GIRM and their titles (with the 1969 and 2002 enumerations) are as follows:

1. The Importance and Dignity of the Eucharistic Celebration (nos. 1–6 [16–26₂₀₀₂])

2. The Structure of the Mass, Its Elements and Its Parts (nos. 7–57 [27–90₂₀₀₂])

3. The Duties and Ministries in the Mass (nos. 58–73 [91–111₂₀₀₂])

4. The Different Forms of Celebrating Mass (nos. 74–252 [112–287₂₀₀₂])

5. The Arrangement and Furnishing of Churches for the Celebration of the Eucharist (nos. 253–80 [288–318₂₀₀₂])

6. The Requisites for the Celebration of Mass (nos. 281–312 [319–51₂₀₀₂])

7. The Choice of the Mass and Its Parts (nos. 313–25 [352–67₂₀₀₂])

8. Masses and Prayers for Various Circumstances and Masses for the Dead (nos. 326–41 [368–85₂₀₀₂])

To these original eight chapters, the 2000 and 2002 revisions of the GIRM added one additional chapter (thereby increasing the total number of paragraphs in the GIRM to 399):

9. Adaptations within the Competence of the Bishops and the Conferences of Bishops (2002 GIRM 386–99)

In comparison with the *Rubricae Generales* and the *Ritus Servandus* of the 1570 Missal, the 1969 GIRM was pastoral and theological in orientation, repeatedly highlighting the truth that it is the entire people of God[8] who together celebrate the Eucharist, under the presidency of a bishop or a priest (1969 GIRM 7 [27₂₀₀₂], 60 [93₂₀₀₂]).

Chapters 1 and 2 in particular address the "why" of the various elements in the liturgy. For example, sections in these chapters remind us that "When the Sacred Scriptures are read in the Church, God himself is speaking to his people" (1969 GIRM 9 [29₂₀₀₂]), that "great importance should be attached to the use of singing in the celebration of the Mass" (1969 GIRM 19 [40$_{2002}$]), that one purpose of the entrance song is to "intensify the unity of those who have assembled" (1969 GIRM 25 [47$_{2002}$]).

Chapter 2, in addition, provides an overview of the parts of the Mass (1969 GIRM 24–57 [46–90$_{2002}$]), leaving the rubrical details to chapter 4. Chapter 3 then addresses the duties of the participants at the eucharistic celebration and is particularly noteworthy because of the special attention given to the "people of God" (1969 GIRM 62 [95–97$_{2002}$]), in contrast to the *lack* of acknowledgement of the assembly in the former *Ritus Servandus.*

Chapter 4 presents the details about various forms of celebration, including Mass with a Congregation but without a deacon (1969 GIRM 77–126 [115–70$_{2002}$]); Mass with a deacon (1969 GIRM 127–41 [171–86$_{2002}$]); Mass with a subdeacon (1969 GIRM 142–152; these original paragraphs were later replaced by sections dealing with the functions of acolytes and readers [187–98$_{2002}$]); concelebrations (1969 GIRM 153–208 [199–251$_{2002}$]); Mass without a congregation (1969 GIRM 209–31 [252–72$_{2002}$]); and general rules for all Masses (1969 GIRM 232–39 [273–80$_{2002}$]), including information about Communion under both kinds (1969 GIRM 240–52 [281–87$_{2002}$]).[9]

Chapter 5 addresses the design of a church and the arrangement of the sanctuary, in particular noting that the "altar should be built free-standing to allow the ministers to walk around it easily and Mass to be celebrated facing the people" (1969 GIRM 262 [299$_{2002}$]). It addresses the placement of chairs for the presiding priest and people, the design of the ambo and its location in the sanctuary, the location of the choir, the location of the tabernacle in the church, and the use of sacred images.

Chapter 6 gives details about the items needed for the celebration, such as the bread and the wine, noting that even though the bread is unleavened, the "meaning of the sign demands that the material for the eucharistic celebration truly have the appearance of food" (1969 GIRM 283 [321$_{2002}$]), the liturgical vessels, the vestments, and their colors. (Some of the details referring to the vestments found in the *Rubricae Generales* section of the 1570

Missal and some of the details referring to the bread and wine found in the *De Defectibus* section were included in an abbreviated form in this chapter.)

Finally, chapters 7 and 8 address which Mass texts are to be used and how to make a choice when several options are possible. Noteworthy is the admonition that "in planning the celebration of Mass, then, the priest should pay attention to the common spiritual good of the people of God, rather than his own inclinations" and that "choices are to be made in consultation with those who perform some part in the celebration, including the faithful" (1969 GIRM 313 [352$_{2002}$]).

Conclusion

The intense work by members of the Consilium, aided by consultation with bishops and scholars,[10] produced a revised Order of Mass along with a guiding document, the GIRM, that was faithful to the vision of the Constitution on the Sacred Liturgy and was generally well received by priests and lay people alike. Unlike the preliminary documents found in the 1570 Roman Missal that were not changed for centuries, the GIRM was destined for several revisions over a relatively short period of time.

Notes

[1] See Joseph A. Jungmann, S.J., *The Mass of the Roman Rite: Its Origins and Development* (New York: Benzinger Bros., 1959) 102. A more detailed history of the *Ordines* may be found in Eric Palazzo, *A History of Liturgical Books from the Beginning to the Thirteenth Century* (Collegeville: The Liturgical Press, 1998).

[2] There were minor changes introduced in 1604 by Clement VIII, in 1634 by Urban VIII, and in 1914 by Pius X. See Jungmann, *The Mass of the Roman Rite* 106 and Robert Cabié, *The Church at Prayer,* vol. 2, *The Eucharist* (Collegeville: The Liturgical Press, 1986) 176.

³ For details, see Annibale Bugnini, *The Reform of the Liturgy 1948–1975* (Collegeville: The Liturgical Press, 1990). This well-done volume by someone intimately connected with the liturgical reforms provides an in-depth view of the process from someone who directed much of the revision. Chapter 5 (pp. 49–53) speaks about the Consilium itself and chapter 12 (pp. 137–98) gives an overview of the various meetings held.

⁴ As noted earlier, references to earlier editions of the GIRM will be to the 1975 text, which is the commonly available version found at the front of current sacramentaries. As also noted earlier, the 2002 GIRM uses a single numbering throughout, starting with the introduction, introduced in the 1970 Missal, and renumbers the paragraphs found in the previous versions of the GIRM. This renumbering was necessitated by the addition of new paragraphs and the omission of paragraphs deemed no longer necessary. When helpful, the older numbering will be included in brackets with a subscript to the 1975 (or other) text, e.g., 2002 GIRM 16 [1₁₉₇₅] indicates paragraph 16 of the 2002 GIRM which corresponds to paragraph 1 of the 1975 GIRM.

⁵ One should not overlook the alternative tradition, followed by many Eastern Churches, of priest and people together facing the east in prayer. This is the posture advocated by Joseph Cardinal Ratzinger in *Spirit of the Liturgy* (San Francisco: Ignatius Press, 2000) 74–84.

⁶ Concerning why this is still "ideal": The ambo is primarily associated with the *ministerial* function of proclaiming the Scripture (2002 GIRM 59 [34₁₉₇₅], 309 [272₁₉₇₅]) and, if there are readers and a deacon (or a concelebrant) present at Mass, there is no necessity for the priest celebrant to go to the ambo for the proclamation of the Scripture. The homily is part of the *presidential* role of the celebrant (Intro. to the Lectionary, nos. 38, 41) and thus it is "ordinarily" given by the priest celebrant (2002 GIRM 66 [42₁₉₇₅]). Since the presidential chair is associated with the presidential role of the priest celebrant (2002 GIRM 310 [271₁₉₇₅]), it is appropriate for him to preach the homily at the chair. For similar reasons, the *Ceremonial of Bishops* indicates that the bishop should give the homily at the *cathedra* (no. 142).

For the profession of faith, the 2002 GIRM assumes the priest will be at the chair, since the creed is not mentioned concerning what may be done at the ambo (no. 309 [272₁₉₇₅]) and the 2002 GIRM explicitly states that the celebrant is at the chair for the general intercessions (nos. 71, 138). There may be reasons why this ideal "choreography" presented in the GIRM is not observed at some Masses or in some churches. If there is no deacon (or concelebrant), the celebrant must go from the chair to the ambo for the proclamation of the gospel. If a deacon or concelebrant preaches the homily, the ambo is the logical place to use. If the ambo is located closer to the assembly than the chair in the apse, then the ambo, rather than the chair, may be the better location in that church for the celebrant to give the homily (and the 2002 GIRM permits this: no. 136 [97$_{1975}$], 309 [272$_{1975}$]; see also *Ceremonial of Bishops,* no. 142). Thus, it may happen that what "usually" takes place in a specific church (because of a lack of ministers or the physical arrangement of the sanctuary) may not exactly correspond to the ideal of the GIRM. Nevertheless, the general principle that the celebrant's place is at the presidential chair for the introductory rites and the entire Liturgy of the Word still holds.

[7] Although formerly the assembly (or servers) recited the last petition of the Lord's Prayer, *sed libera nos a malo,* the prayer itself was considered a *prex sacerdotalis.* In a 1968 reply to the United States bishops, the Holy See noted that the Lord's Prayer had become a communitarian prayer through the rubrical changes in the late 1960s. See the *Newsletter* of the U.S. Bishops' Committee on the Liturgy (BCL) 5, no. 2 (1969). This shift from a priestly prayer to the communal prayer was informally anticipated by the instruction of the Congregation of Rites, *De Musica Sacra et Sacra Liturgia* (3 September 1958), which permitted the entire congregation to recite the entire text of the Lord's Prayer (in Latin) in unison with the priest at a "low" (i.e., recited) Mass (no. 32).

[8] The use of the term "people of God" is ambiguous in that, following chapter 2 of the Dogmatic Constitution of the Church *(Lumen Gentium)* of Vatican II, the term often properly refers to all the baptized, whether ordained or not. Such is the way "people of God" is used in 1969 GIRM 1 [16$_{2002}$] and 7 [27$_{2002}$]. In contrast, in 1969 GIRM 62 [95–97$_{2002}$], "people of God" is used in distinction to the ordained mentioned in 1969 GIRM 59–61 [92–94$_{2002}$].

[9] The sections of the GIRM pertaining to Concelebration and Communion under Both Kinds were actually minor revisions of the rubrics published 7 May 1965 by the Congregation of Rites.

[10] See Bugnini, 942–52 for a list of members of the Consilium, of the consultors, and of advisors. Chapter 13 (pp. 199–202) discusses the non-Catholic observers whose input was solicited, and chapter 14 (pp. 205–18) addresses the letters sent to presidents of episcopal conferences to obtain worldwide input.

CHAPTER 3

Evolution of the GIRM
What has been done? (continued)

The 1970 GIRM and Roman Missal

Although the revised Order of Mass and the GIRM appeared publicly in late 1969, the complete revised Roman Missal itself did not appear until 26 March 1970. The complete Missal contained the revised texts of the presidential prayers, the liturgies of Holy Week, the liturgies of other special days (e.g., Ash Wednesday, the Presentation of the Lord), and other auxiliary rites (the blessing and sprinkling of water in place of the act of penitence). It also included a collection of new "solemn blessings" to be used, optionally, on major feasts and at special, more solemn celebrations. In addition, new sets of prayers were composed, for example, for the section Masses for Various Needs and Occasions. Some of these new texts, such as the Mass for the Progress of Peoples, were based on conciliar texts from Vatican II and on other magisterial statements. Finally, several changes were introduced into the 1969 version of the GIRM.

Some of the changes in the GIRM were relatively minor, such as including the incensation of the host and chalice when they are shown to the people during the institution narrative (1970 GIRM 235e [$276e_{2002}$]),[1] mentioning the optional use of the *Sanctus* bell before the consecration (1970 GIRM 109 [150₂₀₀₂]), and introducing certain changes that were of the nature of clarifications or corrections in terminology. Certain other changes, however, were more substantial.

Although reports had circulated about the revision of the Mass for several years, some people, including two cardinals, Alfredo Ottaviani and Antonio Bacci, were shocked when the texts appeared in 1969 and vocally complained that the revised Order of Mass was a break with the tradition of the Church.[2] In response, a special introduction to the GIRM was written and included in the 1970 Missal and is, in effect, a defense of the Apostolic Constitution of Pope Paul VI approving the revised Missal. This introduction tried to address the concerns that had been raised about the changes in the Mass in its three major sections:

1. A Witness to Unchanged Faith (nos. 2–5)

2. A Witness to Unbroken Tradition (nos. 6–9)

3. Accommodation to Modern Conditions (nos. 10–15)

This introduction argued that, contrary to the concerns raised, the revisions were actually very much in continuity with the past and were an appropriate response to the modern world.

In addition, certain paragraphs in the body of the 1969 GIRM were revised in response to worries expressed that the original texts did not convey the traditional Catholic theology of the Mass. As a result, significant changes were introduced into numbers 7, 48, 55d, 60 (2002 GIRM nos. 27, 72, 79d, 93),[3] and in certain other places. For example, the 1969 GIRM, in describing the parts of the eucharistic prayer, reads as follows:

> 55d: *The narrative of the institution:* in the words and actions of Christ, the Last Supper is made present at which Christ the Lord himself instituted the sacrament of his passion and resurrection, when under the species of bread and wine he gave to his Apostles his Body and Blood to eat and drink, and left them the command to perpetuate this same mystery.

This was changed in 1970 to include the words "consecration" and "sacrifice" and to delete "the sacrament of his passion and resurrection" as follows:

> 55d: *The narrative of institution and the consecration:* in the words and actions of Christ, the sacrifice is carried out which Christ himself instituted at the Last Supper, when, under the species of bread and wine, he offered his Body and Blood, gave them to his Apostles to eat and drink, and left them the command to carry on this same mystery. (See 2002 GIRM 79d)

Similarly, other changes introduced classical terminology at other points of the GIRM.

The Revision of Minor Orders and the 1973 GIRM

On 15 August 1972, Pope Paul VI issued two documents, the *motu proprio Ministeria Quaedam,* which revised the former "minor orders," and the apostolic letter *Ad Pascendum,* which addressed norms for the diaconate. Two results of these documents were the suppression of the major order of subdeacon and the expansion of the duties of the acolyte to include giving Communion as an extraordinary minister. As a result, the texts of the GIRM were emended in 1973 to omit references to the subdeacon (e.g., 1970 GIRM 65, 81c, 142–52, 301) and to add references to the general duties of the acolyte (1973 GIRM 65 [98_{2002}]), to cleansing the chalice (1973 GIRM 238 [279_{2002}]), and to assisting with Communion under both kinds (1973 GIRM 244–52; see [284_{2002}]).[4]

The Second Edition of the Roman Missal and the 1975 GIRM

With a decree dated 27 March 1975, the second edition of the Roman Missal was promulgated. Once again the GIRM was updated, this time in several ways.

For example, sections that had been deleted in 1973 because of the suppression of the subdiaconate were replaced by sections dealing with the ministry of the acolyte (1975 GIRM 142–47

[187–93₂₀₀₂]) and the ministry of the reader (1975 GIRM 148–52 [194–98₂₀₀₂]). To clarify the naming of the bishop in the eucharistic prayer, a section from a 1972 decree about how to include the name of the bishop of the diocese and, optionally, of any auxiliary or other bishop was added to the 1975 GIRM 109 [149₂₀₀₂]. Some of the Roman documents and rites that had appeared since the first edition of the Missal were reflected in revised footnotes and other textual additions, such as the explanation in the 1975 GIRM 11 (see [31₂₀₀₂]) that introductions to the people need not always be spoken verbatim.

A few changes in terminology were also introduced into the 1975 GIRM which are appropriate to note. For example, the word used to describe the lifting of the consecrated host and chalice during the institution narrative of the eucharistic prayer was changed from "elevation" *(elevatio)* to "showing" *(ostensio)* (1975 GIRM 109, 233, 235e [150, 274, 276e₂₀₀₀]).[5] The word "celebrant" was changed or expanded to "priest" *(sacerdos)* or "priest celebrant," particularly in the section on Communion under both kinds.[6]

There were numerous other minor changes in the GIRM in terminology, mainly for the sake of consistency or clarification, as well as additions and changes in the texts and rubrics in the body of the Missal itself. For example, every preface was given a summary subtitle, and several new Masses were added, such as for the Blessing of Abbots and Abbesses, for the Dedication of a Church, for the Dedication of an Altar, and in honor of Mary, the Mother of the Church. Also added were entrance and Communion antiphons for Masses for which none had previously existed.[7]

The Promulgation of the Revised Code of Canon Law and the 1983 GIRM

The revised Code of Canon Law *(Codex Juris Canonici, CIC)* was promulgated on 25 January 1983. The 1983 CIC addresses topics related to the celebration of Mass, such as the homily, concelebration, the reservation of the Eucharist, the architecture of churches (including the construction of altars), and the bread and wine used for the Eucharist. For this reason, on 12 September 1983, a list of "Variations" was published which introduced several minor changes in the text of the GIRM in several numbers and footnotes. The GIRM was changed where it referred to the homily, concelebration, the altar, the tabernacle, the bread for Mass, and Masses celebrated without an assembly, so that the text of the GIRM followed more closely the text found in the 1983 CIC.[8]

Notes

[1] The incensation of the host and chalice after each consecration was standard in the Tridentine Missal, but was not listed in the 1969 GIRM among the points when incense could be used.

[2] See Annibale Bugnini, *The Reform of the Liturgy 1948–1975* (Collegeville: The Liturgical Press, 1990) 277–301.

[3] See *Notitiae* 6 (1970) 169–93 for the complete list of changes. *Notitiae* was the official publication of the Concilium and has become the publication of the Congregation for Divine Worship and Discipline of the Sacraments. Most of the major changes were reported in the BCL *Newsletter* 6, nos. 7–8 (1970).

[4] See *Notitiae* 9 (1973) 34–38. Some omitted sections were not immediately replaced with new texts until 1975. The major changes were reported in the BCL *Newsletter* 9, no. 3 (1973).

[5] The word "elevate" is used during the eucharistic prayer now for the lifting up of the paten with the consecrated bread and the chalice during the final doxology (2002 GIRM 151, 180), a gesture formerly called the "minor elevation."

[6] The Latin text of the GIRM is careful, as is the Latin of the Code of Canon Law and the *Catechism of the Catholic Church* (e.g., in no. 1530), in its use of *sacerdos* and *presbyter,* both of which are often rendered by the same English word, "priest." There is an important technical difference that is lost when one English word is used to translate these two Latin words. *Sacerdos* refers to the one who can preside at a *sacrificium* (sacrifice), and therefore refers both to a bishop and a *presbyter* (priest). *Presbyter* refers to someone who has been ordained to the second grade of the sacrament of holy orders.

[7] See *Notitiae* 11 (1975) 290–337.

[8] See *Notitiae* 19 (1983) 540–43. The numbers that were affected were 1983 GIRM 42, 153, 155, 211, 242, 255, 262, 265, 266, 267, 277, 282, and footnotes 44, 62, 82, and 89.

CHAPTER 4

The 2000 and 2002 GIRM and the Third Edition of the Roman Missal
What is being done?

Much has happened in the over twenty-five years since the last complete edition of the Missal appeared in 1975. For example, Eucharistic Prayers for Reconciliation and for Masses with Children appeared provisionally in 1974, but afterwards were definitively approved for general use. The Eucharistic Prayer for Various Needs was published in a definitive Latin edition in August 1991 for eventual inclusion in the next edition of the Missal. In fact, this prayer was a revision of the prayer created for the Swiss Synod in early 1974.[1] The second edition of the Lectionary was published with a revised introduction in 1981, and the *Ceremonial of Bishops* (CB) was published in 1984 with subsequent changes introduced in reprintings in 1985 and 1991. Each had implications for the Roman Missal. In addition, many had pointed out that various sections of the existing GIRM were inconsistent or anachronistic in light of thirty years of experience, for example, the prohibition against women entering the sanctuary (1975 GIRM 70) or the detailed instructions on distributing Communion from the chalice using a tube or a spoon (1975 GIRM 248–52).

Early in 2000, the Vatican announced that a third edition of the Roman Missal would be published with a revised GIRM. A revised text of the GIRM was then made public in late July 2000, but the actual publication of the complete third edition of the Roman Missal with the definitive revision of the GIRM in Latin was delayed until March 2002. In retrospect, the delay was fortuitous since, after the publication of the 2000 GIRM, various inconsistencies were noticed in that text. As a result, when the third edition of the Missal appeared in 2002, the text of the GIRM was emended in over 210 of the 399 paragraphs as well as in a number of footnotes. In many cases, the changes pertained to questions of capitalization, punctuation, spelling, or grammar in the Latin, or a consistent use of terminology, or the addition, modification, or correction of footnotes. Since there were only a few major changes between the 2000 and 2002 editions (mainly in a complete revision of nos. 256–58, dealing with the beginning of a "private" Mass), the following comments about the changes introduced in 2000 should be understood as also applying to the 2002 GIRM; thus, cross-references will be to the 2002 GIRM.

The changes introduced into the GIRM in the 2000 version fall into six general categories:

1. Editorial Changes

2. Insertions to Correct Inconsistencies

3. Insertions and Emendations Based on Liturgical Documents Issued Since 1975

4. Omissions and Emendations Due to Twenty-Five Years of Experience

5. Additions for Consistency with Recent Liturgical Books

6. Other Changes

Let us now look at each of these categories and at a few examples (far from exhaustive) of the types of changes they represent.

Editorial Changes

As noted above, the introduction to the GIRM was not included when the GIRM and the Order of Mass were first published in

1969 but was added when the complete Roman Missal appeared in 1970. At that time, this introduction was given an independent paragraph numbering. In the recent revision, some outdated paragraphs from earlier versions of the GIRM were deleted from the 2000 GIRM (such as those dealing with where female readers may proclaim the readings and with Communion under both kinds), and other new paragraphs were added. As a result, a renumbering was necessary and a single numbering has now been used for all parts of the 2000 and 2002 GIRM, starting with the introduction. Thus, what used to be no. 1 in the 1969 GIRM is now no. 16 in the 2002 GIRM.

There are some interesting editorial changes in wording. In some cases, the text was changed so that the priest no longer "goes up to" *(ascendit)* the altar but rather "approaches" *(accedit)* the altar.[2] The Book of the Gospels *(liber evangeliorum)* is now referred to by the single Latin word *Evangeliarium*. The readings are proclaimed "from" *(ex)* the ambo, rather than "at" *(in)* the ambo. "Episcopal conference" *(conferentia episcopalis)* is now "conference of bishops" *(conferentia episcoporum)*.

There are other textual changes, seemingly to avoid any possible confusion. For example, references to the "reverence" made toward the altar are made more explicit, by substituting or including "profound bow" *(profunda inclinatio)* where formerly the text merely had "proper reverence" *(debita reverentia)*. References to "ministers" now include "sacred" when the ordained are meant, and references to "acolytes" now include "duly instituted" *(rite institutus)* to avoid confusion with altar servers. (This is the way that acolytes had been designated in the 1984 *Ceremonial of Bishops,* no. 28, as well.) In several places where the former text merely had "says," the revised text now has "sings or says."

There are also places where the text has been reworded and expanded, seemingly to provide clarity. For example, in describing the rite of peace (2002 GIRM 82 [56b_{1975}]), instead of saying that the faithful "offer some sign of mutual charity for each other before sharing in the one bread," the revised text says that the faithful "express some sign of their ecclesial communion and mutual charity for each other before receiving sacramental Communion." Although the former text appropriately used the biblical image of "one bread," the revised text provides a link between the "ecclesial communion" expressed in the rite of peace and the "sacramental Communion" soon to follow.

Correcting Inconsistencies

Whereas the previous general description of parts of the Mass in chapter 2 (1975 GIRM 24–57) overlooked the presence of the deacon, the revised text (2002 GIRM 46–90) mentions the deacon when appropriate, making this description generally harmonize with the rubrics given in the Order of Mass itself. The 1975 GIRM made no reference to the blessing and sprinkling with holy water in place of the act of penitence. That is now included in 2002 GIRM 51. The omission of mention of the Holy Spirit in key places has been corrected making the revised text explicitly Trinitarian (2002 GIRM 16, 78, 79c; cf. [1, 54, $55c_{1975}$]).

The previous version of the GIRM was inconsistent about including the people's responses in the instructions. Often it did (1975 GIRM 86, 112, 115, 124 [124, 154, 157, 167_{2002}]), and sometimes it did not (1975 GIRM 95, 108 [134, 148_{2002}]). The revision has attempted to include the people's responses consistently throughout. References to incensing the altar now also mention incensing the cross to be consistent with 2002 GIRM 277 (cf. [236_{1975}]).

Insertions and Emendations Based on
Other Liturgical Documents

Since the 1975 second edition of the Roman Missal was published, there have appeared the rites of dedication of a church and an altar (1977), the *Graduale Romanum* (1979, containing the revised *Ordo Cantus Missae*), the second edition of the Lectionary (1981), the Code of Canon Law (1983), and the *Ceremonial of Bishops* (CB, 1984) in addition to other documents, letters, and instructions (e.g., *Inaestimabile Donum* [1980]). The revised GIRM has been influenced by all of these.

For example, 2002 GIRM 298 (in contrast to [261$_{1975}$]) notes that the altar is a symbol of Christ (see Dedication of a Church, no. 16a). A new paragraph on silence during the Liturgy of the Word (2002 GIRM 56) is taken almost verbatim from the second edition of the introduction to the Lectionary (no. 28) along with a paragraph about the dignity of the Lectionary and the Book of the Gospels (2002 GIRM 349; see Intro. Lectionary, no. 35).

In the 2000 GIRM, the sequence was specified as being sung *after* the Alleluia (no. 64) to correspond to what appeared in *Ordo Cantus Missae* (no. 8). This, however, was one of the items changed in the 2002 GIRM, so that the text now prescribes the sequence to be sung *before* the Alleluia, the order in which they appear in most printed editions of the Lectionary.

More detailed instructions[3] on how to incense (2002 GIRM 277) are taken from the *Ceremonial of Bishops* (nos. 91–93) along with details about the general intercessions (2002 GIRM 138; see CB 144) and the regulation that one does not genuflect before the tabernacle when walking in procession (2002 GIRM 274; see CB 71).

The prohibition against the tabernacle being on the altar on which Mass is celebrated (2002 GIRM 315) is taken from the 1967 document *Eucharisticum Mysterium* (EM, On the Mystery of the Eucharist, no. 55), a regulation also repeated in the 1973 section of the Roman Ritual, "Holy Communion and Worship of the Eucharist Outside of Mass" (Intro., no. 6). This regulation is similar to the prohibition in the *Ceremonial of Bishops* against bishops celebrating Mass at an altar at which the Blessed Sacrament is reserved with the prescription that the reserved Sacrament should be transferred to another place if Mass must be celebrated at such an altar (CB 49).

The exhortation that priests should celebrate Mass daily (2002 GIRM 19) is taken from the Code of Canon Law (can. 904) and found in *Eucharisticum Mysterium* (no. 44).

The new paragraph (2002 GIRM 305) on the use of flowers during Advent (in "moderation") and Lent (prohibited except on

Laetare Sunday) is also based on norms in the *Ceremonial of Bishops* (CB 48, 236, 252).

Omissions and Emendations Due to Twenty-Five Years of Experience

The comments in 1975 GIRM 70 about permitting women to proclaim Scripture readings were anachronistic and have been dropped (cf. 2002 GIRM 107). The detailed instructions, which first appeared in 1965 when Communion under both kinds was initially allowed, about how to minister Communion from the chalice via a straw ("tube") or using a spoon (1975 GIRM 248–52) have also been deleted since these methods were probably never used in the last thirty-five years anyway. The details about Communion via intinction remain since this method, although symbolically less perfect than drinking from the chalice, has been in long use in some Eastern Catholic Churches and is common in some other countries.

There are other emendations that seem to respond to pastoral practice developed over the last thirty years. For example, the 2002 GIRM no longer demands the use of the chalice veil, but notes that its use is "laudable" (no. 118). The 2002 GIRM now permits the homily to be given either at the chair or the ambo or "in another suitable place" (no. 136). At the invitation to Communion *(This is the Lamb of God),* the priest may, as an alternative to holding a piece of the broken eucharistic bread over the paten, hold it over the chalice (2002 GIRM 84, 157, 243, 268), a welcome alternative especially when Communion is distributed under both kinds (as is encouraged by 2002 GIRM 85, 282).

Health is cited as a reason why someone might not kneel during the consecration (2002 GIRM 43). Whereas the 1975 GIRM (nos. 178, 182, 186, 190) seemed to restrict which parts of the eucharistic prayer could be sung, the 2002 GIRM now explicitly permits any part "for which musical notation is provided" to be sung (no. 147). The 2002 GIRM now acknowledges that tabernacles often are found on old altars in sanctuaries (no. 315), sometimes centered behind the altar used for Mass (no. 310). Thus it states that as an alternative to a separate eucharistic reservation chapel, the Eucharist may be reserved in the sanctuary, but it explicitly leaves the ultimate determination as to where to reserve the Eucharist to the diocesan bishop.

There have been subtle changes in the rules for Communion under both kinds that suggest that the revised GIRM now envisions the practice as commonplace and presumes that someone other than the presiding priest will also be receiving from the chalice at every Mass. The 1975 GIRM, no. 242, listed fourteen cases when Communion could be distributed under both kinds "at the discretion of the Ordinary and after prerequisite catechesis." The corresponding paragraph in the 2002 GIRM, no. 283, omits this condition, thus implying that one no longer needs explicit permission of the ordinary to offer Communion from the chalice in the cases mentioned. This revised paragraph makes a general reference to cases mentioned in ritual books (e.g., RCIA, confirmation, marriage) and includes a reduced list consisting of three categories: (1) priests who are not concelebrating; (2) the deacon and others performing some duty at Mass (e.g., readers, eucharistic ministers); and (3) everyone present at a community Mass, all seminarians, all retreatants, and all participating in a pastoral meeting. In addition, the diocesan bishop may now allow Communion under both kinds in other situations, without reference to guidelines and restrictions promulgated by the conference of bishops (as had been specified in 1975 GIRM 242). Although the list is shortened, the categories of individuals who may receive Communion from the chalice have actually been increased, and the norm is reworded so that those mentioned in the GIRM are given permission, by liturgical law, to receive Communion from the chalice at Mass, rather than merely being offered this form of Communion only at the explicit determination of the diocesan bishop.

Major Additions

Many of the new and revised introductions to liturgical books and rites include a final section addressing adaptations permitted by the conferences of bishops. Such a new section (chapter 9, 2002 GIRM nos. 386–99) has been included in the revised GIRM.

This chapter summarizes the decisions found elsewhere in the GIRM that can be made by conferences of bishops or individual bishops and summarizes principles and procedures found in the 1994 Roman instruction on the liturgy, The Roman Liturgy and Inculturation *(Varietates Legitimae)*.

Other Changes

There are other interesting additions and changes to the GIRM which do not quite fit into the five previous categories. These other changes fall into about five additional categories and a few examples of each of these types are presented without attempting to be exhaustive.

1. Some additions do not change existing practice, but merely make explicit what should be done.

For example, the 2002 GIRM adds that the priest is bound to receive the Eucharist from what has been consecrated at the same Mass (no. 85, see also no. 243) but puts this in the context of the faithful receiving Communion from what has been consecrated, emphasizing even more strongly that one should not use the Eucharist reserved in the tabernacle during Mass unless absolutely necessary.

The 2002 GIRM states that it is desirable to celebrate Mass facing the people whenever possible (no. 299).[4]

The custom of celebrating three Masses on the Commemoration of All the Faithful Departed (All Souls) has been explicitly included in the list of when the celebration or concelebration of Mass more than once a day is permitted (2002 GIRM 204d).

There is explicit mention that other priests, deacons, or extraordinary ministers may assist the presiding priest in distributing Communion (2002 GIRM 162, 182).

There is also a note about what to do with any consecrated eucharistic bread remaining after Communion: It may be consumed or brought to the place of reservation (2002 GIRM 163).

There is a note that when there is no deacon at a concelebration at which a bishop is the principal celebrant, a priest who proclaims the Gospel should ask a blessing from the bishop (2002 GIRM 212; see CB 74). The text also notes that a priest should not ask for a blessing if the principal celebrant is another priest.

II. Other additions may change established practices in some places since the earlier versions of the GIRM were interpreted in a broader fashion.

The 2002 GIRM now explicitly notes that the "altar cross" is to have "the figure of Christ crucified upon it" (nos. 117, 308).

The 2002 GIRM specifically notes that the Lectionary is never carried in procession (no. 120d), only the Book of the Gospels, paralleling the practice of the Byzantine Liturgy. The 1975 GIRM similarly mentioned the carrying of the Book of the Gospels, but since many countries or small parishes never had a separate Book of the Gospels, the Lectionary was, in practice, often used instead.[5]

Extraordinary ministers of the Eucharist should receive the vessel with the eucharistic species from the hands of the priest (2002 GIRM 162), imitating the practice of priests receiving vessels of chrism when they assist a bishop at a confirmation (*Rite of Confirmation,* no. 28), and they should approach the altar only after the Communion of the priest (2002 GIRM 162).

The 1975 GIRM noted that the priest could extend the sign of peace to the ministers near him (no. 112). But in many places, the priest left the altar area and greeted some in the assembly. The 2002 GIRM specifically notes that the priest should not extend the sign of peace to those outside the sanctuary "so that the celebration not be disturbed" (2002 GIRM 154).

Since the breaking of the bread reflects one of the key verbs used in the New Testament to describe the actions by Jesus at the Last Supper, the rite of breaking the bread is now explicitly reserved to the priest and the deacon (2002 GIRM 83).

III. Yet other additions emphasize good liturgical practice.

The 2002 GIRM includes new paragraphs pertaining to the altar that emphasize the respect due the altar. They emphasize that only what is necessary should be on the altar table, explicitly noting that flowers should not be placed on top of the altar (2002 GIRM 305–6). Even when a priest celebrates Mass with only one minister assisting, the readings should be proclaimed at the ambo or a lectern (2002 GIRM 260).

If there is a tabernacle in the sanctuary, one does not genuflect before it during the celebration of Mass, but only when first arriving at the sanctuary during the entrance procession and when leaving after the dismissal (2002 GIRM 274).

The practice of the assembly joining the priest in praying the concluding doxology of the eucharistic prayer *(Through him, with him, in him)* had already been discouraged by the 1980 instruction, *Inaestimabile Donum* (no. 4) when it noted that "It is an abuse to have some parts of the Eucharistic prayer said by the deacon, by a lower minister or by the faithful. . . . The *Per Ipsum* itself is reserved to the priest." The substance of this prohibition is now emphasized in the 2002 GIRM where it notes that the "Eucharistic Prayer demands, by its very nature, that the priest alone speak it" (no. 147) and that "The concluding doxology of the Eucharistic Prayer is spoken solely by the principal priest celebrant and, if desirable, together with the other concelebrants, but not by the faithful" (no. 236).

Since every sacramental action is a gift ministered by someone else, *Inaestimabile Donum* (no. 9) also prohibited the faithful from self-communicating at Mass and this prohibition has also been explicitly included in 2002 GIRM 160.[6]

IV. Other changes permit new practices within the celebration of the Mass.

A bishop is now permitted to bless the assembly with the Book of the Gospels after the proclamation of the Gospel (2002 GIRM 175), imitating a long-standing practice at papal Masses and in some usages of the Byzantine Rite.

As an alternative to a triple swinging of the censer, the priest is permitted to incense the bread and wine at the preparation of the gifts by making a single sign of the cross over the gifts with the censer (2002 GIRM 277).

As noted earlier, the former list of cases when Communion under both kinds may be given is reduced to three categories (2002 GIRM 283) no longer needing the explicit permission of the diocesan bishop. The GIRM then refers to other cases mentioned in other ritual books. In addition, it also permits the diocesan bishop to establish additional norms regarding when Communion may be distributed from the chalice. As noted above, even though the number of categories listed has been reduced, these changes do not restrict the instances when Communion may be received from the chalice, but actually presuppose a more general practice.

V. A few changes actually alter what the current legislation prescribes.

Omitting the psalm on weekdays when the *Alleluia* is sung is no longer an option (2002 GIRM 63a [cf. 38a$_{1975}$]).

The section on posture now says that the assembly stands before they give their response to the *Pray, brethren* introducing the prayer over the offerings (2002 GIRM 146 [107$_{1975}$] and 2002 Order of Mass 29).[7]

Some other changes will be noted in the evaluatory comments in the next chapter.

The 2002 GIRM, the Order of Mass, and the Roman Missal

As noted earlier, in a number of paragraphs of the 2002 GIRM, changes had been introduced into corresponding paragraphs of the earlier 2000 GIRM making terminology, spelling, or capitalization consistent in the Latin text, and a few additional footnotes were added. A few of the more significant changes include the following:

1. Kneeling after the *Agnus Dei* is noted as a permitted posture, if the conference of bishops so determines (2002 GIRM 43).

2. The location of the sequence vis-à-vis the *Alleluia* has been changed from *after* the *Alleluia* (2000) to *before* the *Alleluia* (2002 GIRM 64).

3. It is explicitly noted that the offertory chant (or approved alternative) may be sung even if there is no procession with the gifts (2002 GIRM 74).

4. An explanation for the commingling is given, saying that it signifies the unity of the Lord's Body and Blood, living and glorious, in the work of salvation (2002 GIRM 83).

5. The purpose of the dismissal has again been noted (i.e., reinserting, as 2002 GIRM 90c, the explanation found in 1975 GIRM 57b, which had been omitted in the 2000 GIRM).

6. The reference to cleansing the vessels after Communion at the "side of" the altar has been omitted (2002 GIRM 163).

7. It is explicitly noted that the priest must hold a host *consecrated at that Mass* when inviting the assembly to Communion (2002 GIRM 157).

8. The rubrics of the introductory rites for a Mass celebrated with only one minister assisting have been changed, explicitly noting that the greeting and the act of penitence normally take place at the *chair* rather than near the altar although the priest and server may chose to remain at the altar after its initial veneration (2002 GIRM 256–58).

9. The use of "more precious" vestments at more solemn celebrations has been once again permitted (i.e., reinserting, as 2002 GIRM 346g, the norm of 1975 GIRM 309, which had been omitted in the 2000 GIRM).

10. Concelebrants may sing or say the concluding doxology of the eucharistic prayer along with the principal priest *if it seems desirable* (i.e., reinserting the permission since the late 1960s of allowing the principal celebrant to say or sing the doxology *alone* without the concelebrants, a practice which seems to have been eliminated in 2000 GIRM 236).

The rubrics of the Order of Mass in the 2002 Missal remain substantially the same as in the 1975 Missal. In a few cases, the text has been expanded to correspond to what appears in the 2002 GIRM. The *only major difference* is that the rubrics of the Order of Mass explicitly permit the use of the Apostles' Creed in lieu of the Nicene Creed whenever the profession of faith is required, especially during Lent and the season of Easter. The option of using either form is not mentioned in the GIRM since it only uses the general terms of "symbol" or "profession of faith."

The 2002 Missal itself includes various new prayers and minor textual and rubrical changes. For example, separate prayers over the people for optional use on each day of Lent have been included as well as a text for the solemn proclamation on the Epiphany of the dates of moveable feasts.[8] In addition, some prayer texts have been edited and minor revisions introduced. For example, Eucharistic Prayer II for Masses with Children was noteworthy because of a lack of reference to the Holy Spirit in the first epiclesis. That omission has now been corrected and the phrase "by the power of the Holy Spirit" has been introduced into the Latin text. Other minor textual changes have been introduced into the Eucharistic Prayers for Masses of Reconciliation as well. Clarifying rubrics, repeating the norms found in the GIRM, have now been included at the beginning of the sections containing Votive Masses, Masses for Various Needs and Occasions, and Ritual Masses to note explicitly on which days such Masses are permitted. As an example of a rubrical change, at the Easter Vigil, the rites related to inscribing the candle after the blessing of the new fire are no longer listed as optional, and the first proclamation of *Light of Christ* is specified as taking place when the procession reaches the entrance to the church (rather than before it leaves the location of the new fire). The introduction to the Eucharistic Prayers for Masses of Reconciliation now explicitly includes a rubric saying that although these prayers have proper prefaces, they may be used with other penitential prefaces, such as those for Lent.

Notes

[1] See *Notitiae* 27 (1991) 388–478.

[2] In two cases, namely in 2002 GIRM 123 and 173, changes introduced in 2000 were actually changed back in 2002 when the sense of the paragraph meant going from the level of the assembly to the level of the sanctuary, which is supposed to be "elevated" (2002 GIRM 295).

[3] Because of a lack of directions about incensation in the 1969 GIRM, some priests continued to use, for example, the elaborate triple crosswise and triple circular incensations during the preparation of the gifts that were prescribed by the 1570 Missal. Such elaborate gestures did not seem to harmonize with the "noble simplicity" mandated by the Constitution on the Sacred Liturgy (no. 34). The new paragraphs about how to incense do add a new level of detail, but also clarify the gestures and prescribe a simplicity that is in contrast with the rules of the 1570 Missal.

[4] The seemingly absolute statement of the 2002 GIRM was clarified by an interpretation issued by the Congregation of Divine Worship and Discipline of the Sacraments on 25 September 2000. This clarification states that, although facing the people is desirable, the phrase "whenever possible *(ubicumque possibile sit)*" means that celebrating Mass facing the apse is "not excluded."

[5] The symbolism of honoring Christ present in the gospel narratives, the basic reason for the ancient tradition of carrying the Book of the Gospels alone in the entrance procession, was obscured when some parishes had a server carry the Sacramentary, a reader carry a Lectionary, and the deacon carry the Book of the Gospels. Only a single book, if any, should be carried in the entrance procession, and the ancient tradition is that this book be the Book of the Gospels.

[6] See Robert Taft, S.J., "Receiving Communion—a Forgotten Sign," *Worship* 57 (1983) 412–18. Taft notes that eighth-century documents indicate that even at a papal Mass, the pope was given Communion by someone else.

[7] There seems to be a slight inconsistency since 2002 GIRM 43 [21$_{1975}$] says that the assembly stands "from the invitation, *Pray, brethren*." It is consistent for the GIRM to have the people standing whenever they are reciting something in common (except for the response, *Thanks be to God,* after the first two readings). But it is usually difficult for any large group to begin reciting a common text after changing posture without someone to lead them. Thus, in practice, in some places it may happen

that the priest may gesture to the assembly to stand *before* he begins the invitation to prayer (so they can begin their response immediately without a change in posture) or the assembly may continue the current practice of changing posture only *after* they have finished their response.

[8] The formal proclamation of the dates of moveable feasts had been included in the 1984 Italian *Messale Romano* (BCL *Newsletter* 20, nos. 4–5 [1984]) and is mentioned in the *Ceremonial of Bishops* (no. 240). It was also included in the Sacramentary supplement published in the United States in 1994.

CHAPTER 5

General Evaluation

Nearly thirty years passed between the previous edition of the Roman Missal, which appeared in 1975, and the publication of the third edition of the Missal in 2002. Given this length of time and the number of liturgical documents that had appeared during that more than a quarter of a century, in addition to the new saints added to the calendar, it should be acknowledged that it was time for an updated edition of the Roman Missal to be issued along with a good editing of the GIRM. To a great extent, the revised GIRM (along with the minor changes, clarifications, and additions to the rubrics in the Order of Mass) is an improvement over the previous version by including information not readily available before, clarifying rubrics, emphasizing even more good liturgical practices, and permitting new options. The vast majority of changes can be considered improvements, especially in light of pastoral experience with the 1969 Order of Mass for over thirty years.

Some of the major liturgical themes that have been emphasized in a positive way in the 2002 GIRM include silence, singing, symbolism of liturgical objects, Communion from what is consecrated at that Mass, Communion under both kinds, and the unity of the assembly. These and a few other topics will be discussed in more detail in chapter 7, in the context of what communities should focus on when evaluating the liturgical experience in their churches and chapels. Unfortunately, such fundamental liturgical aspects and principles will probably continue to be overlooked in spite of the renewed emphases on them.

Yet, some people may judge the tone of other places in the document to be less positive than hoped for in this revision, and there are new specifications that seem more restrictive than necessary.[1] In addition, some may be disappointed that various topics discussed in the early 1990s, when the work was begun on the third edition of the Roman Missal, were not incorporated.[2]

For example, there is a new sentence about "laudably retaining" the practice of kneeling from the *Sanctus* to the end of the eucharistic prayer and after the *Agnus Dei* (2002 GIRM 43) and about the deacon kneeling "as a rule" during the epiclesis and institution narrative of the eucharistic prayer (2002 GIRM 179). For those who feel that standing is a more ancient and appropriate posture for Christian prayer when the community gathers to remember the risen Lord, such directives about kneeling may seem a step backwards and unnecessarily restrictive, although they are in keeping with the traditional practices of the Roman Rite and coincide with the piety of many of the faithful.[3]

In places where local practices have developed over the last thirty years—based on the common interpretation of the 1969 GIRM—for example, where the priest greets some of the faithful during the sign of peace or the eucharistic ministers assist during the breaking of the bread, the new rubrics that specify that the priest should remain in the sanctuary during the sign of peace (2002 GIRM 154) and that restrict the rite of breaking the bread to the priest and deacon (2002 GIRM 83) may also seem unnecessary. It also seems unnecessary to require the priest or deacon alone to consume all the remaining Precious Blood (2002 GIRM 163, 182, 247), and to require the vessels to be cleansed "immediately" after the dismissal of the people (2002 GIRM 163). It seems odd to prohibit the proclamation of a single reading by several readers (2002 GIRM 109), especially since this latter was encouraged by the Directory for Masses with Children (DMC 47). It also appears odd to specifically prohibit the substitution of other hymns for the *Gloria* and *Agnus Dei* (2002 GIRM 53, 366) although such substitutions have not been a wide-spread practice in the U.S.

Yet one should not be too quick to dismiss the revised rubrics in the 2002 GIRM without trying to understand the underlying vision. The fundamental vision in the 2002 GIRM is the same vision that was portrayed in the Constitution on the Sacred Liturgy and in the original 1969 GIRM. It is a vision of God's people, united in prayer, led by a presiding bishop or priest, giving glory to God, through Christ, prompted by the Spirit. Those who remember the first Mass in English in the fall of 1964 may remember the awkwardness of praying publicly in our native languages. The transitions to a vernacular eucharistic prayer, to additional eucharistic prayers, and then to a new Order of Mass in the late 1960s and early 1970s also were marked by a certain awkwardness. As with any transition, sometimes incorrect choices were made and less than ideal practices were established without proper reflection. Some of the changes in the 2002 GIRM can be viewed as attempts to include "correctives" to practices that, perhaps, are more significant than might appear to many.

For example, the specification that the priest remain in the sanctuary for the sign of peace presupposes an underlying context. The rite in the 1969 Order of Mass is seen as an activity in which everyone shares the peace of the risen Lord with those around them, whomever they may be. It is a sign of "ecclesial communion and mutual charity before receiving sacramental Communion" (2002 GIRM 82, cf. [$56b_{1975}$]). In the 1570 Missal, the peace started with the priest kissing the altar (thereby receiving peace from the symbol of Christ), who gave it to the deacon, who gave it to the subdeacon, who gave it to the senior acolyte, and so on. The 1969 Order of Mass deliberately changed the older, clerical, "trickle-down" form of the rite and opted for a communal rite in which all simultaneously give and receive Christ's peace from their neighbors. In actuality, the 1969 GIRM never suggested that the priest should greet the people. The text said that the priest may give the sign of peace "to the ministers" (1969 GIRM 112 [154_{2002}]) or the deacon to "other ministers closer to him" (1969 GIRM 136 [181_{2002}]).

Although an "extended" rite of peace may be, at other times, very appropriate, one can rightly criticize any liturgical action that is out of proportion, considering its location in the complete liturgy. In a prolonged rite of peace, there is a danger of reintroducing elements of the older clericalism of the rite of peace if the assembly were to wait until the priest greeted them before greeting one another or if the priest went through the entire assembly. There is also a danger of making this preparatory rite, which should signify "ecclesial communion" more important than the "sacramental Communion" that follows, if it should be very lengthy. Thus it seemed desirable to attempt to correct what may seem to be aberrations. Hence, the GIRM suggests that the reason the priest should not leave the sanctuary is so that "the celebration not be disturbed" (2002 GIRM 154). One may disagree with the restriction, but the underlying principles and vision are well worth considering!

As another example, the norms that extraordinary ministers of Communion not approach the altar before the priest has received Communion and should receive the vessels of the Eucharist from the presiding priest (2002 GIRM 162) may seem impractical.[4] Yet one could rightly question the appropriateness of the practice of having extraordinary ministers receive Communion and function during the Communion rite as if they were concelebrating priests. Some practices introduced over the last few decades may actually have introduced a new clericalism rather than merely permitting lay people to exercise an appropriate ministry in the local church.

Others may question new determinations that may seem somewhat arbitrary, because, in some instances, one or another norm may pertain to a relatively new practice in the Roman Rite. For example, in several places in the 2002 GIRM, there is a note that the excess sacred elements (in particular, the Precious Blood) are consumed at the altar (2002 GIRM 163, 182, 247, 279), contrary to the practice of the Byzantine Rite in which the excess consecrated elements are always consumed at the separate table of preparation after the liturgy.[5] Elsewhere, the 2002 GIRM stipulates that auxiliary ministers of the Eucharist should not approach the altar until after the Communion of the priest (2002 GIRM 162). Also, the

2002 GIRM now specifies that the altar cloth should be white (2002 GIRM 304, cf. [268₁₉₇₅]), contrary to the practice of many Eastern Catholic Churches.

One may also detect a subtle shift in the tone of the 2002 GIRM by an increased number of references to priests and what they should do. Although the 1983 CIC notes that priests should celebrate Mass daily, this text is now explicitly included in 2002 GIRM 19. The 1967 instruction *Eucharisticum Mysterium* suggested that it is preferable for priests to concelebrate rather than attend Mass (EM, 43, 47) and this has been explicitly included in 2002 GIRM 114 (cf. [76₁₉₇₅]). The new prescriptions that the priest should not leave the sanctuary during the kiss of peace, that auxiliary ministers of the Eucharist receive the vessels from the priest celebrant, that the priest consumes the remaining Precious Blood also seem to shift the focus from the assembly during the celebration of Mass, to the leader of its prayer.

These and other changes may cause consternation to some people, but one should remember that, in general, the rubrics have not changed substantially, and there is more to make use of in the GIRM to encourage *good liturgical practices* than there is to bemoan.[6]

Notes

[1] See the detailed analysis of the 2000 GIRM by Carlo L. Braga, C.M. in *Ephemerides Liturgicae* 114 (2000) 481–97. There the author wonders about the necessity of changes such as the detailed rubrics regarding the hands during the final blessing (2002 GIRM 167), the necessity of requiring a white altar cloth, the omission of permission to use more precious vestments on festive days (changed in the 2002 GIRM), the necessity of having an image of the crucified on the cross (contrary to the old traditions of a "glorious" or "jewelled" cross), and other textual changes. Also see the careful article by John M. Huels in *Worship* 75 (2001) 482–511, in which he addresses changes in the 2000 GIRM in terms of subsidiarity or uniformity.

[2] See *Notitiae* 27 (1991) 38ff.

[3] In fact, it is the practice of various Eastern Catholic Churches, even in the United States, always to *stand* at prayer, especially on Sundays. The 20th canon of the Council of Nicaea, in 325, prescribed standing at prayer on Sundays and during the Easter Season and, earlier, Tertullian (second to third centuries) forbade fasting and kneeling on Sundays since it was a sign of penance (*De corona militis,* 3, 4).

[4] The shift in when extraordinary ministers come to the altar is also seen in the revision of the brief rite for commissioning an extraordinary minister for a single occasion, found as one of the appendices of the Missal. The previous version prescribed that such extraordinary ministers come to the priest during the *Agnus Dei* and were blessed for their ministry before the invitation to Communion. The revised version in the 2002 Missal now states that they come only after the priest finishes receiving Communion.

[5] The GIRM does seem, at times, to treat the credence table in a way very similar to the *proskomedia* (preparation) table of the Byzantine Rite. For example, the chalice is to be at the credence table, not at the altar, when Mass begins (2002 GIRM 118c [$80c_{1975}$]); the deacon may prepare the chalice at the side table rather than at the side of the altar (2002 GIRM 178 [133_{1975}]), thereby more correctly postponing the placement of the chalice on the altar until *after* the *Blessed are you* prayer of the presiding priest (see 2002 GIRM 75 [49_{1975}]); and it is preferred that the cleansing of the vessels take place there as well (2002 GIRM 279 [238_{1975}]).

[6] See Bishop Donald Trautman's address, "Liturgical Renewal: Keeping the Virtue of Hope," *Origins* 32 (2002) 256–60. One must also remember that the way one interprets liturgical and canon law is not the same as the way one follows U.S. law. One example of this difference can be seen in the clarification of 25 September 2000 concerning 2002 GIRM 299 and its phrase "which is desirable whenever possible" referring to the altar separated from the wall and celebrating Mass facing the people. The response from the Congregation of Divine Worship and the Discipline of the Sacraments, signed by its prefect, Cardinal Jorge Medina, stated that the text of the GIRM *does not exclude* the possibility of celebrating Mass "facing the apse." The response makes reference to various circumstances of the place and of those present. Thus even though the text seems quite clear in recommending the celebration of Mass facing the people, an official clarification seems to backtrack. Nevertheless, what is interesting and worthy of reflection by all is the final sentence of the explanation: "Taking a rigid position and absolutizing it could become a rejection of some aspect of the truth which merits respect and acceptance."

CHAPTER 6

The U.S. Adaptations to the GIRM and the Norms for Communion Under Both Kinds

In accordance with 2002 GIRM 390 (see also [6₁₉₇₅]), national conferences of bishops have the right (and in some cases the obligation) to make certain decisions pertaining to the celebration of the Eucharist and may include such decisions within their national vernacular edition of the Missal. Ever since 1970, U.S. editions of the Order of Mass or of the complete Sacramentary have included an appendix that indicated the decisions of the U.S. Conference of Bishops pertaining to the celebration of Mass for the Church in the United States. Similar appendices exist in the missals of other countries, for example, the "precisions" found in the 1984 edition of the Italian *Messale Romano*.[1] The decisions contained in such an appendix modify the GIRM for the country for which they were intended. The Congregation for Divine Worship and the Discipline of the Sacraments now prescribes that any national adaptations be included as part of the actual text of the GIRM for that country, so that one need not check in several different locations in the book to see what is actually permitted in that country. Thus the English text of the 2002 GIRM as published in the U.S. may, in the future, be different in specific places from the versions published in England or Canada. In each case, that version of the GIRM is binding for the celebration of the Mass in that country.

The more significant decisions formerly contained in the U.S. appendix, in most cases in effect since 1969, and which now have been incorporated into the 2002 GIRM, include the following:

- Establishing guidelines concerning what is sung at the entrance, after the first reading, during the preparation of the gifts, and during Communion, and what types of musical instruments may be used including a required review of the settings of certain liturgical texts set to music (2002 GIRM 48, 61, 87, 393 [26, 36, 56i, 275$_{1975}$][2]).

- Modifying the GIRM's norm regarding the posture of the assembly (2002 GIRM 43 [21$_{1975}$]).

  (In contrast with the provisions in the GIRM which prescribes kneeling during the eucharistic prayer only for the epiclesis and consecration, the U.S. bishops retained the practice of kneeling, as a rule, from after the *Sanctus* until the end of the doxology. In addition, in 2001 the U.S. bishops explicitly determined that the assembly kneel after the *Agnus Dei,* during the invitation to Communion, *This is the Lamb of God* but gave the diocesan bishop authority to determine otherwise.)

- Permitting Communion in the hand and extending permission when Communion could be ministered under both kinds (2002 GIRM 160 [117, 240$_{1975}$]; the former reference to 1975 GIRM 242 is no longer needed under the provisions of 2002 GIRM 283).

- Permitting the use of white vestments for funeral Masses and Masses of the dead, and gold or silver vestments on special occasions (2002 GIRM 346 [308$_{1975}$]).

- Leaving specific determinations up to the local diocesan bishop when there is doubt about the suitability of nontraditional materials, such as the material for altars, vessels, vestments, and liturgical furnishings, and when days of prayer should be scheduled (2002 GIRM 301, 326, 329, 373 [263, 288, 290, 331$_{1975}$][3]).

- Implementing the Lectionary for Mass fully and allowing certain changes in the readings (2002 GIRM 362).

Additional new decisions approved by the U.S. bishops in June 2001 (and confirmed by Rome in March 2002) include the following:

- Permitting the priest, in special circumstances, to extend the sign of peace to some members of the assembly near the sanctuary (2002 GIRM 154).

- Determining that in the United States, Communion is to be received standing and that the gesture of reverence before receiving Communion is a bow of the head by the communicant (2002 GIRM 160).

- Referring to using the *Norms for the Celebration and Reception of Holy Communion Under Both Kinds in the Dioceses of the United States of America* (2002 GIRM 283).

- Allowing other colors for altar cloths beneath the top white cloth (2002 GIRM 304).

- Specifying the type of vesture used by lay ministers (2002 GIRM 339).

- Specifying special days of prayer including 22 January as a day of prayer for life (2002 GIRM 373).

In addition, when the U.S. Conference of Bishops first extended permission to minister Communion under both kinds on Sundays, they created a *directory* (a document containing "directions"), entitled *This Holy and Living Sacrifice* (THLS), which also became liturgical law in the United States. This directory, confirmed by Rome in 1984, was revised in light of the 2000 GIRM, approved by the U.S. bishops in June 2001, and retitled *Norms for the Celebration and Reception of Holy Communion Under Both Kinds in the Dioceses of the United States of America*. In particular, these norms explicitly state that where there is need, the eucharistic

ministers may consume whatever remains of the Precious Blood
(Norms 52; see 2002 GIRM 163, 182). In response to a request for
an indult, Rome also granted permission for eucharistic ministers
to assist in cleansing the vessels after Communion (2002 GIRM
279).[4]

The U.S. bishops also approved the *optional* veiling of crosses
and images during the end of Lent, a decision confirmed by Rome
in 2002. Since this practice is not mentioned in the GIRM, the
mention of the U.S. practice will eventually be found in the same
place where the mention of the practice is found in the Latin edition of the Missal, namely before the liturgical texts for the Fifth
Sunday of Lent.

When the revised translation of the second edition of the Roman
Missal was being examined by the U.S. bishops in 1995, other
variations were also proposed, such as explicitly allowing the assembly to raise their hands in the ancient *orans* gesture during the
Our Father (as is commonly done in Italy), moving the sign of
peace to before the preparation of the gifts (as is common in the
Ambrosian Rite of Milan), and permitting kneeling during the
penitential rite during Lent.[5] It is possible for these and other minor
national adaptations to the Roman Missal and the GIRM to be introduced in the future. The existence of these and other variations
point out that the GIRM is a living document, providing general,
worldwide norms for everyone using the Roman Mass but also
permitting appropriate adaptations that respond to national pastoral needs and cultural sensitivities. Such adaptations are the
major concern of the new chapter 9 in the 2002 GIRM, the chapter on adaptations.[6]

It is also appropriate to acknowledge the existence of the "Pastoral Introduction" to the Roman Missal as modified for the U.S.
This document, in the style of the expanded pastoral notes found
in the *Pastoral Care of the Sick, The Order of Christian Funerals,*
and *The Rite of Christian Initiation of Adults,* summarizes the
various directives from the GIRM and other sources (e.g., *Ceremonial of Bishops*) in a format somewhat more "user-friendly"
than what is found in the GIRM (in which the same information

may be contained in numerous locations under various section headings). It also offers sound pastoral advice to help all involved in the liturgical life of the local community to prepare prayer-filled liturgies that can nourish the spiritual life of those present.[7]

Notes

[1] See BCL *Newsletter* 5, no. 12 (1969) for the original list of decisions for the U.S. See vol. 20, nos. 4–5 (1984) for a report on the Italian *Messale Romano*.

[2] The earlier U.S. appendix also had an explicit reference to 1975 GIRM 50 [74$_{2002}$], which addressed the chant used at the preparation of the gifts. This paragraph of the GIRM refers to the earlier paragraph that deals with the chant used during the entrance procession, so specific guidelines for that number are not needed.

[3] The earlier U.S. appendix also had an explicit reference to 1975 GIRM 305 [343$_{2002}$], which addressed the materials used for vestments and permitted the use of synthetic and other cloths for vestments. No reference to this number appeared in the documentation made public by the U.S. Catholic Conference of Bishops in 2002.

[4] It is odd that this indult seemed necessary, since when a question about whether eucharistic ministers could help cleanse the vessels was raised in 1978, the Congregation for Divine Worship and the Discipline of the Sacraments determined that what applied to acolytes also applied to extraordinary ministers in this matter. *Notitiae* 14 (1978) 593–94.

[5] See BCL *Newsletter* 31 (1995) 15–19.

[6] Although the Constitution on the Sacred Liturgy prohibits additions, deletions, or changes in the liturgy on anyone's own initiative (CSL 22, see also 2002 GIRM 24; based on Pius XII's *Mediator Dei*, 20 November 1947, no. 109), such prohibitions should be interpreted "strictly" (see CIC 18). On the one hand, it would be incorrect, for example, to make use of the maniple again, since the 1969 GIRM definitively dropped the mention of this vestment in revising the Order of Mass, and it would be contrary to the vision of the current Roman Missal to add something that had been consciously removed. On the other hand, certain new practices may be in the spirit of the current Missal, though not explicitly mentioned, for example, the practice of Communion ministers receiving the

Eucharist at the end of the Communion rite and being sent forth formally from the assembly to the sick and homebound of the community. This latter practice was given tacit approval by the *Circular Letter Concerning the Preparation and Celebration of the Easter Feasts,* no. 53 (16 January 1988). The 1975 GIRM never explicitly permitted auxiliary Communion ministers (lay or ordained) to assist the celebrant during the Communion rite, yet no one doubted that this practice was permitted. New practices and new forms of devotion in the Catholic Church have arisen throughout the ages because, generally, liturgical law favors the principle that "what is not prohibited is permitted" (see BCL *Newsletter* 6, no. 11 [1970]), a principle that is found in the Roman legal tradition in various forms from the third century (see the *Digest of Justinian,* 1, 5, 4 prol.). As was noted by a Vatican official, some rubrics should be seen as *descriptive* rather than *proscriptive* (see Helen Hull Hitchcock, "New Liturgy Rules Precede Missal," *Adoremus Bulletin* 6, nos. 6–7 [2000]). Interpreting liturgical law is often more difficult than interpreting civil laws, for example regarding driving, because of the nuances of obligations found in the liturgical norms. See John M. Huels, *Liturgical Law: An Introduction* (Washington: The Pastoral Press, 1987) or Ronald F. Krisman, "Father (Always?) Knows Best: A Pastoral Interpretation of Liturgical Norms," *AIM: Liturgy Resources* 31, no. 4 (2002) 13–16.

[7] The Pastoral Introduction was originally written in the 1990s by the International Commission on English in the Liturgy (ICEL) to be included in the revised translation of the second edition of the Roman Missal. When the third edition of the Roman Missal appeared, this introduction was revised and adapted by the U.S. Bishops' Committee on the Liturgy with the U.S. in mind, and issued as a separate companion guide to the Missal.

CHAPTER 7

The Future
What should be done?

The command recorded by the Synoptic Gospels as being uttered by Jesus at the Last Supper was "Do this in memory of me" (Luke 22:19). From the earliest days of the Church, the Christian community gathered for prayer and for the "breaking of the bread" to fulfill the Lord's command (Acts 2:42). In the sharing of the one loaf and the one cup, they recognized their unity in the risen Lord (1 Cor 10:17), a unity so dearly prayed for by the Lord before he died (John 17:21).

The celebration of the Eucharist constitutes the Church and it is the duty of all Christians, by reason of their baptism, to celebrate the Eucharist to the best of their abilities, with that "full, conscious, and active participation" so desired by the Second Vatican Council (CSL 14). It is important to remember that the celebration of the Eucharist or of any other sacrament or liturgical rite, is not an end in itself, but only a privileged means of deepening our union with God and our love for our sisters and brothers in Christ as we continue on our earthly pilgrimage to our heavenly home. Our liturgical celebrations are a way of helping us, young and old, female and male, ordained and lay, worship our God who touched our world in the person of Jesus, his Son. That Son reminded us that love of God should be reflected in love of neighbor and of self. The noted American Episcopalian liturgical historian Thomas Talley wisely noted: "Too many communities have already been brought to despair by the discovery that, having rearranged the furniture of the sanctuary and instituted an offertory procession, they still don't love one another."[1] No matter how rubrically correct a liturgy is, if it has not in some way helped those assembled experience a *metanoia,* deepened their union with and love of our triune God, and led them to help God's kingdom of love and justice become more of a reality in our world, something has been missing from that liturgy. As we reflect on the 2002 GIRM and on how our community celebrations of the Eucharist live up to the ideals depicted in it, we must remember the ultimate reasons why we gather to celebrate the Eucharist at all!

In the statement *Music in Catholic Worship,* of the U.S. Bishops' Committee on the Liturgy, we read, "Good celebrations foster and nourish faith. Poor celebrations may weaken and destroy it" (no. 6). Our constant challenge, in liturgy as in all of life, is to get some perspective, and then to evaluate what are strengths and what are weaknesses, what are lights and what are shadows. Then aided by the norms, insights, and principles found in the GIRM, we can continually work to improve our celebrations, in order to better "foster and nourish" the faith of those present.

Although some may suggest that some of the changes in the 2002 GIRM are overly restrictive, it is important to note the fundamental liturgical principles it still upholds and emphasizes even more than before. It will be easy for people to become preoccupied by the differences between the 1975 GIRM and the 2002 GIRM and, perhaps, even easier for some to fixate on what seem to be new restrictions. But we should remember that the Lord castigated those who wanted to "strain out the gnat and swallow the camel" (Matt 23, esp. vv. 4, 23, 24). It is more important to use the publication of the third edition of the Roman Missal with the 2002 GIRM as a time to reflect on the basic liturgical principles that the 2002 GIRM emphasizes, and also to engage in a sort of "examination of conscience" as to how well the communities to which we belong are guided by these fundamental principles. The publication of the 2002 GIRM and the eventual publication of revised vernacular Missals in English and other languages provide the Church an opportunity for catechesis and private study about liturgical principles as well as for some changes in practices, if such are actually needed.

Perhaps focusing on a few such fundamental principles incarnated in the 2002 GIRM can stimulate reflection on the common practices we see in our parishes.

The Unity of the Assembly

In describing the duties of the bishop at a Eucharist, the 1975 GIRM (no. 59) noted that the Church is "the sacrament of unity." This phrase provides the basis for the revised version of the opening paragraph of chapter 3 (2002 GIRM 91 [58_{1975}]) which speaks of the eucharistic celebration as an action of Christ and "a holy people united to and ordered under the Bishop." Because of a past piety that is often described as an individualistic "Jesus and me" spirituality, and because of cultural forces that emphasize a "rugged individualism," the call to unity, which has been a part of the GIRM since 1969, has often gone unheeded. The GIRM cautions against "any appearance of individualism or division" (2002 GIRM 95 [62_{1975}]) and encourages all to form "one body" (2002 GIRM 96 [62_{1975}]) in the celebration of Mass.

At the beginning of the description of the liturgy, the GIRM notes that the purpose of singing during the entrance procession is to "intensify the unity of those who have assembled" (2002 GIRM 47 [25_{1975}]). The unity of all assembled is also mentioned in reference to the breaking of the bread (2002 GIRM 83 [$56c_{1975}$]) and the form of the eucharistic bread (2002 GIRM 321 [283_{1975}]). It is mentioned in reference to the posture of those assembled and to communal gestures (2002 GIRM 42, 96 [20, 62_{1975}]). It is even mentioned in reference to the design of a church (2002 GIRM 294 [257_{1975}]).

The reoccurring exhortation to unity should be a challenge for each community to reflect on how well they have responded to Christ's last prayer, "Father, may they all be one" (John 17:21, author's rendering). When people sit scattered throughout a large church, when some are singing and others are not, when some stand after Communion and sing while others kneel and pray silently, even individualistically, the unity that is envisioned in the GIRM is imperfectly symbolized.

Silence as Integral to a Liturgical Celebration

The Constitution on the Sacred Liturgy referred to reverential silence during the liturgy (CSL 30), and the 1975 GIRM included some guidelines about appropriate moments for silence during the Mass (1975 GIRM 23), in particular noting the appropriateness of silence at the end of a reading and of the homily. The 2002 GIRM repeats these original guidelines (2002 GIRM 45), but adds an additional paragraph on silence (taken from the Introduction to the Lectionary, no. 28) during the Liturgy of the Word (2002 GIRM 56), which repeats the same advice.

The thrust of these two paragraphs on silence should challenge us particularly to reflect on how well we provide appropriate moments of reflective silence during our liturgical celebrations. During Masses in our churches, is there a moment of silence after the first reading, or does the reader or cantor rush into the psalm before the people are finished with their *Thanks be to God*? Does the presiding priest allow a moment of reflective silence after the homily so that people can savor the message preached, or does he rush immediately into the profession of faith or the general intercessions? Is there a recognizable moment of silence after the *Let us pray* that introduces the collect and the prayer after Communion, or does the priest celebrant rush immediately into the *O God* that begins the text of the prayer? Are prayers pronounced, by all in the assembly, with a pace appropriate to their dignity, or is the pace closer to that of an experienced auctioneer during an auction? It is so easy to allow the "rat-race" culture in which we live to influence how we celebrate the Eucharist. If anything, we need to provide opportunities for more, rather than less, silence during our celebrations.

Dignity and Symbolic Nature of Liturgical Objects

The 2002 GIRM now points out the ancient tradition of the altar representing Christ, the Living Stone (2002 GIRM 298, also see *Built of Living Stones* [BLS] 56). Ultimately, it is because the altar is the architectural symbol of Christ in a church that it is kissed by the priest and deacon at the beginning and end of a eucharistic liturgy (as well as at other solemn rites, such as Evening Prayer; see CB 196). As a result of this basic symbolism, only those things necessary for the liturgy should be placed on the altar and only when needed.

The 2002 GIRM specifically notes that only the Book of the Gospels should be on the altar before the proclamation of the Gospel, and only the bread and wine and items absolutely necessary (e.g., corporal, purificator, Missal) during the Liturgy of the Eucharist (cf. 2002 GIRM 306).[2] This follows the reverential custom in some Eastern Churches in which even the priest's book of prayers is not supposed to be placed on the altar. The 2002 GIRM now specifically notes that flowers are better placed around the altar rather than upon it (2002 GIRM 305) and reiterates permission to place candles around the altar rather than upon it (2002 GIRM 117, 307 [79, 269$_{1975}$]).

The 2002 GIRM also directs attention toward the altar on which Mass is normally celebrated, rather than toward old altars no longer in use. It does this by prescribing that old altars should not be decorated (2002 GIRM 303) and that a cloth should be used on the altar where "the memorial of the Lord" is celebrated (2002 GIRM 304).

In addition, the 2002 GIRM includes a new paragraph (2002 GIRM 349), taken from the Introduction to the Lectionary (no. 35), that points out that the liturgical books, particularly the Book of the Gospels and the Lectionary, are signs and symbols of transcendent realities and must be dignified and beautiful.

Furthermore, the 2002 GIRM, in two places (2002 GIRM 58, 260), notes that the readings are to be proclaimed from the ambo (a simple lectern is permitted at a Mass with only one minister present). This reemphasizes the admonitions originally found in the 1969 GIRM about the use of the ambo only by those who proclaim God's Word (i.e., deacons, readers, psalmists) and about the dignity of God's Word (1969 GIRM 272 [309$_{2002}$]). The main description of the ambo in the GIRM now includes a sentence about the "dignity of the ambo" and notes that this dignity "requires that only a minister of the word should go up to it" (2002 GIRM 309). Thus, it should not be used by others, such as commentators (2002 GIRM 105b).

One should also note that references to "sign" and "symbol" were also present in previous editions of the GIRM, though often overlooked. In reference to Communion under both kinds, the GIRM notes that "Holy Communion has a fuller form as a sign when it is received under both kinds" (2002 GIRM 281 [240$_{1975}$]). And in reference to the eucharistic bread, the GIRM notes that, "even though unleavened . . . the meaning of the sign demands that the material for the eucharistic celebration truly have the appearance of food" (2002 GIRM 321 [283$_{1975}$]).

The new and revised paragraphs offer us the opportunity to reflect on the basic signs and symbols used during the liturgy and on whether our use of them is in accord with the important spiritual realities they symbolize.

Communion *ex hac altaris participatione*

The 2002 GIRM (in no. 85) has modified the encouragement found in the 1975 GIRM (no. 56h) about the faithful receiving Communion from elements consecrated at that Mass, rather than from the tabernacle and, in a sense, has made it even stronger. The revised paragraph adds that "the priest himself is bound" to receive Communion from what is consecrated at that same Mass. It is in this context that the 2002 GIRM repeats the admonition that "it is most desirable" that the faithful also receive Communion from what is consecrated at that Mass. One should note that even though the 2002 GIRM (as did all the earlier versions) specifies that a church have a tabernacle, and the 2002 GIRM now notes that the leftover hosts not used at Communion may be brought to the "place designated for the reservation of the Eucharist" (2002 GIRM 163), nowhere does it hint that it is ever permitted to go to the tabernacle to distribute the sacramental elements reserved there *during Mass.* The section of the Roman Ritual, "Holy Communion and Worship of the Eucharist Outside Mass," notes in its introduction that the primary purpose of reserving the Eucharist is the administration of viaticum and the secondary reasons are the giving of Communion (outside Mass) and adoration of Christ (no. 5).

Even though the admonition that all receive Communion from what has been consecrated at that Mass has been repeated over and over again, in a document from an ecumenical council, namely Vatican II, and in documents from several popes,[3] it is still common practice in many parishes to bring several ciboria of consecrated hosts from the tabernacle to be used by those ministering Communion at Mass. The ideal of eucharistic practice that is preserved on Holy Thursday, which prescribes only one Mass and an empty tabernacle, should be an ideal that we try to attain at every liturgy. Sunday liturgies may present more problems in planning for the number of communicants, but certainly most parishes should have a sense of how many, within a range of about ten people, will receive Communion at weekday Masses. The ideal of all present sharing from the "one loaf" to become one body in Christ (see 1 Cor 10:17; 2002 GIRM 83 [56c$_{1975}$], 321 [283$_{1975}$]) should be something we should strive for at every Mass.[4]

In addition, communities should heed the advice about offering Communion from the chalice *whenever permitted* (cf. 2002 GIRM 85 [56h$_{1975}$]). The GIRM quite strongly states, "It *is most desirable* that the faithful . . . in the instances when it is permitted . . . participate in the chalice" (emphasis added). Elsewhere the GIRM reminds us of the symbolic value of this way of receiving Communion: "Holy Communion has a fuller form as a sign when it is received under both kinds. For in this manner of reception . . . the divine will by which the new and everlasting covenant is ratified in the Blood of the Lord is more clearly expressed" (2002 GIRM 281 [240$_{1975}$]).

It is noteworthy, as mentioned above, that the 2002 GIRM has removed the need for the bishop's explicit permission to give Communion from the chalice to certain participants at Mass (no. 283), thus presenting Communion under both kinds as the expected way that Communion is given during every Mass, at least to certain members of the assembly. The fact that the 2002 GIRM now permits priests to hold the host over the chalice while inviting the assembly to Communion at the *This is the Lamb of God* (2002 GIRM 84, 157, 268) indicates, through symbol, that the assembly is being invited to receive Communion under both kinds. Once again, we are challenged to strive toward the ideal depicted in the GIRM.

Singing as a Fundamental Component of Celebrations

The 2002 GIRM enhances its encouragement of singing (nos. 39–41) by an addition not found in the 1975 GIRM (no. 19). The 2002 GIRM (no. 40) states that, "every care must be taken that singing by the ministers and the people is not absent in celebrations that occur on Sundays and holy days of obligation." In several places the text of the 2002 GIRM has been emended so that the words "sung or" are added to the words "is said," for example, for the *Kyrie* (2002 GIRM 125 [87$_{1975}$]), the *Gloria* (2002 GIRM 126 [87$_{1975}$]), the profession of faith (2002 GIRM 137 [98$_{1975}$]), and the preface (2002 GIRM 216 [168$_{1975}$]). In at least one case "sings or recites" was changed to "sings" (2002 GIRM 79b [55b$_{1975}$], referring to the *Sanctus*).

Although not mentioned in the Missal, one moment for singing associated with Mass that is often overlooked is at the final commendation at the end of a funeral Mass. The original Introduction to the Order of Christian Funerals notes, regarding the song of farewell, that "not only is it useful for all to sing this song, . . . but all should have the sense of its being the high point of the entire rite" (*Ordo Exsequiarum,* no. 10; *Order of Christian Funerals,* no. 147). Yet too often the text of the Song of Farewell is recited or, if sung, it is performed by a soloist instead of being sung by *all present* and experienced as the *high point* of the rite.

There are still many parish churches where there is no singing at some Sunday Masses, often the early ones, or where singing occurs at secondary times, such as during the preparation of the gifts rather than at liturgically key places, such as before the gospel and during the eucharistic prayer. All editions of the GIRM have proclaimed the words of Augustine that "Singing is for lovers" (2002 GIRM 39 [19$_{1975}$]), and if we are to be known as "Christians by our love," we should also be known as Christians by our enthusiasm in singing as well.

Distribution of Ministerial Roles

Although it is not a critical aspect of theology that affects every liturgy, a principle that often tends to be overlooked is the proper delegation and distribution of liturgical roles. The Constitution on the Sacred Liturgy of the Second Vatican Council addressed the issue of the ideal of a community of believers gathered together but, nevertheless, reminded us that all should do their proper roles and not anything more (CSL 28). This principle has been explicitly mentioned in the GIRM twice (2002 GIRM 5, 91 [Intro. 5, 58$_{1975}$]).

One consequence of this principle is that the priest celebrant should not proclaim a Scripture reading when other appropriate ministers are present. Thus, in referring to the function of proclaiming Scripture, the GIRM reminds us that this function "is ministerial, not presidential. Therefore, a reader should proclaim the readings, and a deacon or, in his absence, a priest other than the celebrant should announce the Gospel" (2002 GIRM 59 [34$_{1975}$]). The GIRM also advises that "if there are several readings, it is better to distribute them among a number of readers" (2002 GIRM 109 [71$_{1975}$]).

Since each minister should ideally do only what is part of his or her specific ministry, it is preferable, for example, when capable ministers are available, not to have one person serve as both reader and eucharistic minister at the same Mass.

Regarding the distribution of roles, there is a danger that exists, namely the tendency to delegate too much, as is seen when the principal celebrant delegates the introduction and conclusion of the general intercessions to a concelebrant. Certain parts of the Mass by their nature belong to the principal celebrant and, thus, should *never* be delegated to another (see 2002 GIRM 108). On the other hand, there is also the danger of perpetuating the pre-Vatican II model of the presiding priest being the liturgical *factotum* and reserving several ministerial offices to himself, contrary to liturgical principles (as well as to rubrical norms).

The ideal envisioned by the GIRM is a community of faith with an adequate number of ministers, each of whom performs his or her assigned task during the eucharistic celebration, all in service of the community's worship of God.

The Bishop as Chief "Liturgist" and Liturgical Teacher

The role of the bishop as the primary celebrant of the Eucharist was noted in the 1969 GIRM (no. 59; see [92_{2002}]) in chapter 3 where the duties and roles of ordained and nonordained ministers were discussed. The 1969 GIRM also noted the appropriateness of priests concelebrating with their bishop on major occasions (no. 157 [203_{2002}]). These texts were not newly created in 1969 but they reflect key themes found in various documents of the Second Vatican Council. For example, the Constitution on the Sacred Liturgy reminds us that "the principal manifestation of the Church consists in the full, active participation of all God's holy people in the same liturgical celebrations, especially in the same Eucharist, in one prayer, at one altar, at which the bishop presides, surrounded by his college of priests and by his ministers" (CSL 41). Elsewhere, in the Constitution on the Church, *Lumen Gentium,* we read "every legitimate celebration of the Eucharist is regulated by the bishop, to whom is confided the duty of presenting to the divine majesty the cult of Christian religion" (no. 26; see CB 5–17).

In carrying out this theme found in ancient patristic tradition as well as in recent conciliar decrees, a new paragraph in chapter 1 of the 2002 GIRM (no. 22) reminds us that the bishop is the "moderator, promoter, and guardian" of the liturgical life of the diocese and that it is his duty to help his priests, his deacons, and the faithful of his diocese "always grasp more deeply a genuine sense of the rites and liturgical texts," so that they may be "led to an active and fruitful celebration of the Eucharist." Not only is the bishop described as the one with authority over the liturgy, but he is described as one who should be the model of how to preside at the liturgy, as the one who teaches and leads his fellow ministers and the entire people of God to a deeper experience of the liturgical celebrations. He is the one who does all he can to enhance the "dignity of these celebrations."

Because dioceses in Western Catholicism are generally so large, both in number of people and in territory, most Catholics have never met their bishop and know him only through his first name, mentioned during the eucharistic prayer at Mass. In many parishes, the bishop is a remote figure and may seem to have as much influence in running a small parish as Bill Gates of Microsoft has in running a local computer store. While there is no easy solution to this dilemma, at the same time it should be acknowledged that the liturgical life of the local diocese should draw its strength from its bishop.

In some Eastern Catholic Churches there is often a greater closeness to the bishop, perhaps because the numbers of the faithful and of the clergy are fewer. But there are other reasons that often assist in fostering this unity. Among some groups, for example those who follow some of the older liturgical traditions of the Byzantine Rite, *every* church has a chair reserved for the bishop. The fact that it is empty most often helps to remind those assembled that they are part of a larger community of faith.

One of the beauties of our Catholic tradition is our connectedness. We are not autonomous congregations—or even independent local dioceses or independent national churches. We are part of God's people redeemed by Christ, in whom there is no male or female, no Jew or Greek (see Gal 3:28). Our worldwide unity in Christ is not really based on ideology but ultimately on persons: a local parish united around its pastor; a local diocese around its bishop; several dioceses with their bishops united with the regional archbishop; in some places, a nation united around its primate or patriarch; and all bishops, primates, and patriarchs in communion with the Bishop of Rome. At every level, there is a communion of people and a communion of churches, in the end resulting in a universal communion. It is this personal connectedness of our faith that ultimately reflects the personal way the Lord reached out to the people of his land to heal, to teach, to nourish, and to love.

Notes

[1] Thomas J. Talley, *Worship: Reforming Tradition* (Washington: The Pastoral Press, 1990) 49.

[2] Thus the older practices of putting the veiled chalice on the altar at the beginning of Mass, or of leaving the cruets with water and wine and the bowl for washing hands on the altar, are not allowed and, in effect, are prohibited.

[3] See Dennis C. Smolarski, S.J., *How Not to Say Mass* (Mahwah: Paulist Press, 1986) 58.

[4] The practice of reserving a special host for the priest (often about 2.5 inches in diameter), which is entirely consumed by the presiding priest, needs to be reexamined. Such a practice seems to be in conflict with 2002 GIRM 321 [283$_{1975}$] which states that the eucharistic bread should be made in such a way that the priest can break it into parts "and distribute them to at least some of the faithful." Thus, the GIRM seems to recommend use of larger hosts, often called "concelebration size," as a standard practice. See Dennis C. Smolarski, S.J., *Q&A: The Mass* (Chicago: Liturgy Training Publications, 2002) 45–47.

CHAPTER 8

Final Reflections

One reaction to the third edition of the Roman Missal and the revised 2002 GIRM is to change established practices quickly based on a private interpretation of liturgical norms or on personal piety and without guidance from those more knowledgeable or those in authority. Such an approach is fraught with danger. One lesson that should have been learned in the difficult transition years between the mid-1960s and the mid-1970s is that any transition should be done carefully, intelligently, and with proper catechesis and preparation.

The Code of Canon Law is very wise in its admonition that "In a case of doubt, the revocation of a pre-existing law is not presumed, but later laws must be related to the earlier ones and, insofar as possible, must be harmonized with them" (CIC can. 21) and that "Custom is the best interpreter of laws" (CIC can. 27). There exist established liturgical practices based on the earlier versions of the GIRM that have become commonplace for around thirty years, the length of time that canon law notes that a "custom" obtains the "force of law" (CIC can. 26). Thus, drastic changes should never be introduced based on a naive reading of the revised GIRM. Although "custom" is not specifically defined in the Code of Canon Law, which applies to the Latin Church, the Code of Canons of the Eastern Churches gives a hint of the importance of "custom" in canon 1506, which begins, "A custom of the Christian community, insofar as it corresponds to the action of the Holy Spirit in the ecclesial body."

For example, the 2002 GIRM (and its preliminary 2000 version) states that the breaking of the bread "is reserved to the priest and the deacon" (no. 83). Nevertheless, a clarification from Archbishop Francesco P. Tamburrino, O.S.B., secretary of the Congregation for Divine Worship and the Discipline of the Sacraments, in July 2000 noted that this did not automatically prohibit extraordinary ministers of Communion from pouring the Precious Blood from a flagon into auxiliary chalices used for the Communion of the assembly.[1]

Even though the 2002 GIRM (nos. 163, 182, 247) mentions only priests and deacons as those who may consume any remaining consecrated wine after Communion—and the U.S. Catholic Bishops explicitly sought an indult to permit lay eucharistic ministers to consume whatever remained in their chalices—the response from the Congregation for Divine Worship and the Discipline of the Sacraments was that neither an indult nor permission of the diocesan bishop was needed since anyone, minister or communicant, may help consume whatever remains of the excess species in case of need.[2]

Even though the 2002 GIRM does not mention extraordinary ministers among those who may cleanse the chalices (2002 GIRM 279), neither did previous editions (see [238₁₉₇₅]). Nevertheless, the common practice of Communion ministers cleansing the vessels was justified based on 1975 GIRM 70, which permitted laypeople to "perform all the functions below those reserved to deacons." The substance of this paragraph is again included in 2002 GIRM 107.[3]

It is very easy to view the revised GIRM from a legalistic point of view, common with the Anglo-Saxon common law tradition, and not see that some sections are *descriptive* of common practice rather than *proscriptive,* forbidding every other option.[4] A broader historical perspective suggests that a *sensus fidelium* (sense of the faithful) may, in some instances, lead to rubrics (of lesser importance) eventually being overlooked. Such happened with the rubrics in the 1570 Missal regarding the lighting of the *Sanctus* candle from the consecration until after Communion and the distribution of the *purificatio* (a cup of wine mixed with water) to each of the faithful who received Communion (1570 *Missale Romanum, Rit. Serv.,* viii, 6 and x, 6, 9).

Those who long to return to the pre-Vatican II liturgical style may point to the 2002 GIRM and note that it permits the tabernacle on an old altar in the center of the sanctuary. Those who are sensitive to fundamental liturgical principles will point to the 2002 GIRM and note that it more emphatically encourages ministering Communion to the faithful from what has been consecrated at that Mass and discourages cluttering the altar with whatever is liturgically inappropriate and unnecessary at the moment. Neither group will be completely happy with all aspects of this revised document, but, as noted above, such texts always result from compromises.

Other commentaries will most probably become available to focus in greater depth on one or other aspect of the revised GIRM and the third edition of the Roman Missal. Liturgy, as the Church, is a reality that is *semper reformanda*. The publication of the third edition of the Roman Missal and of the 2002 GIRM offers all involved in worship with an opportunity to reflect, once again, on how well we actually celebrate the mystery of the Eucharist, the center of Christian life. For such an opportunity to reflect on how we gather together to praise our God, we should truly give thanks.

There will be other revisions of the GIRM in the future, if the past is any indicator. The challenge of the people of God is to accept these revisions as road signs helping us on our never-ending journey toward the new and eternal Jerusalem as depicted at the end of the book of Revelation (chapter 21). We need to remember that Revelation depicts heaven as a wedding banquet (Rev 19:9) and the Eucharist is our earthly foretaste of that eternal banquet. Celebrating the Eucharist is the most important activity the Church on earth can do to remind us of who we are as followers of Christ. It is our duty to celebrate it as best we can—and the revised GIRM is there to help those Catholics who are part of the liturgical tradition known as the Roman Rite do just that. It is also our duty not to get sidetracked and let the road signs distract us from remembering what our ultimate destination actually is and from also remembering that our nourishment for the journey should enable us to love God and our neighbor better.

When Jesus appeared to the two disciples on the road to Emmaus, they said to him, "we used to hope that he was the one to redeem Israel" (Luke 24:21, see RSV). These disciples had put their hopes in Christ, but in a way that could not be fulfilled. Yet their hopes were, indeed, to be fulfilled in a way they did not expect, in the burning inside their hearts and in the breaking of the bread (Luke 24:32, 35). Many have repeated the same words, "we had hoped," about liturgical renewal, putting their hopes in various practices or texts.[5] Ultimately, we may find our hopes fulfilled in ways we did not expect, when we focus on the burning inside our hearts and the simplicity of the breaking of the bread.

May the Spirit of the risen Lord guide us on our journey toward that new and eternal Jerusalem!

Notes

[1] For the 2000 clarification about eucharistic ministers pouring the consecrated wine into auxiliary cups, see BCL *Newsletter* 36 (2000) 35. It seems, however, that between August 2000 and March 2002, the Congregation for Divine Worship and the Discipline of the Sacraments determined that it was more significant "at the present moment" to emphasize the distinction between laity and ordained ministers. For this reason, it did not grant permission to dioceses in the U.S. to continue the practice of permitting extraordinary ministers of Communion to assist the priest and deacon in distributing the broken consecrated bread and consecrated wine into auxiliary vessels (see excerpts from Cardinal Jorge Medina's letter of 22 March 2002, BCL *Newsletter* 38 [2002] 64–65).

[2] See excerpts from Cardinal Jorge Medina's covering letter of 22 March 2002, BCL *Newsletter* 38 (2002) 64.

[3] In fact, in 1978, the periodical *Notitiae* published a clarification from the Congregation for Divine Worship and the Discipline of the Sacraments about 1975 GIRM 238 saying that "The remarks on the priest, deacon, and acolyte [about cleaning the vessels] are applicable to an extraordinary minister" (14 [1978] 593–94). Even though the matter of whether an ex-

traordinary minister could assist with the cleansing of eucharistic vessels seems to have been clarified by the Congregation for Divine Worship and the Discipline of the Sacraments in 1978, the U.S. bishops nevertheless requested explicit permission to allow eucharistic ministers to cleanse the vessels. This was granted in 2002 as an indult for a limited period of time by the Congregation for Divine Worship and the Discipline of the Sacraments.

[4] The use of the terms "descriptive" and "proscriptive" were used by a Vatican official in commenting on the norms for posture given in the GIRM (43_{2002}), as reported in Helen Hull Hitchcock, "New Liturgy Rules Precede Missal," *Adoremus Bulletin* 6 (2000). See also f. 6 in ch. 6.

[5] See the foreword to Kathleen Hughes' *Saying Amen: A Mystagogy of Sacrament* (Chicago: Liturgy Training Publications, 1999), in which the author, Gabe Huck, reflects on a homily by Cardinal John Wright at the 1960 North American Liturgical Week in which Cardinal Wright used the refrain *sperabamus* ("we used to hope") over and over again.

Appendix
Major Rubrical Changes

This appendix attempts to summarize the major changes, rubrical and non-rubrical, introduced into the 2002 General Instruction of the Roman Missal and into the Order of Mass in the third edition of the Roman Missal. Of course, rubrical changes comprise only some of the numerous textual changes.

These following abbreviations will be used to indicate the general nature of the change:

S = *specification (clarification of what appeared in the previous GIRM)*

O = *option (indicating a new option not in the previous GIRM)*

C = *change (indicating a rubrical change from what appeared in the previous GIRM)*

Preparations for Mass (with the people)

1. Before Mass, the chalice is put on the side table, with the other necessities. It is a laudable practice, but not required, to cover the chalice with a veil (O) 2002 GIRM 118.

2. The Lectionary is put at the ambo, since this book is not carried in the entrance procession (S) 2002 GIRM 118b, 120d.

3. Enough bread is prepared for all, priest and people, for Communion, since it is highly desirable that the people "as

the priest himself is bound to do" communicate from what
is consecrated at that Mass (S) 2002 GIRM 85, 118c.

4. The altar cloth should be white (S) 2002 GIRM 304.

5. Nothing should be on the altar other than what is necessary, specifically the Book of the Gospels during the Liturgy
of the Word, and the Missal, altar linens, bread and wine
(in appropriate vessels) during the Liturgy of the Eucharist
(S) 2002 GIRM 306.

6. The cross used as the altar cross should have the image of
Christ on it (C) 2002 GIRM 117, 122, 308. (There is no
mention, however, of the processional cross having to have
a corpus [2002 GIRM 119, 120b], unless it is used as the
altar cross [2002 GIRM 122].)

The Order of Mass (with the people)

1. The Book of the Gospels, but not the Lectionary, may be
carried in the entrance procession (S) 2002 GIRM 120d, 172.

2. Whenever the Book of the Gospels is carried in procession, it is to be slightly elevated (S) 2002 GIRM 120d,
133, 172, 175.

3. If the tabernacle is in the sanctuary, the priest and ministers genuflect to it when arriving at the sanctuary and at the
end of Mass, but not during Mass (S) 2002 GIRM 274.

4. It is preferable that different readers proclaim different
readings, but each reading is proclaimed by a single reader
(S) 2002 GIRM 109.

5. On a weekday, the psalm should not be omitted if the
Alleluia is sung (as in 1975 GIRM 38a). The psalm and
Alleluia may be combined by using *Alleluia* as the refrain
(C) 2002 GIRM 63a.

6. The sequence is sung before the Alleluia (S to GIRM, C to
Ordo Cantus Missae) 2002 GIRM 64.

7. After the proclamation of the gospel, a bishop may bless the assembly with the Book of the Gospels (O) 2002 GIRM 175.

8. In addition to being at the chair or at the ambo, the homilist may also preach from another suitable place (O) 2002 GIRM 136.

9. The Apostles' Creed is permitted as an option to the Nicene Creed, especially during Lent and the Easter season (O) 2002 Order of Mass 19.

10. Singing during the preparation of the gifts may take place even if there is no procession (S) 2002 GIRM 74.

11. For the incensation of the gifts, the presiding priest may either incense the gifts with three swings of the censer or make a sign of the cross with the censer over the gifts once (O) 2002 GIRM 277.

12. The people should stand after the priest's invitation to pray, *Pray, my brothers and sisters* and before the response, *May the Lord* (S) 2002 GIRM 146, 2002 Order of Mass 29.

13. It is explicitly noted that the bishops of a country may permit the practice of kneeling from the end of the *Sanctus* to the end of the eucharistic prayer (C) 2002 GIRM 43.

14. "Reasons of health" is stated as a reason why people might not kneel at prescribed moments of the liturgy (O) 2002 GIRM 43.

15. The priest may sing any part of the eucharistic prayer for which music is provided (C) 2002 GIRM 147.

16. The deacon normally kneels during the institution narrative (S) 2002 GIRM 179.

17. If the assembly remains standing during the eucharistic prayer, they should bow while the priest genuflects after the consecrations (S) 2002 GIRM 43.

18. The faithful are not to say the concluding doxology of the eucharistic prayer with the priest (S) 2002 GIRM 236.

19. The priest should not leave the sanctuary at the kiss of peace (S) 2002 GIRM 154.

20. The breaking of the bread is reserved to the priest and deacon (S) 2002 GIRM 83.

21. It is explicitly noted that the bishops of a country may permit the practice of kneeling from after the *Agnus Dei* to the beginning of the Communion procession (C) 2002 GIRM 43.

22. The priest may hold the host over the chalice when inviting the assembly to Communion at the *This is the Lamb of God* (O) 2002 GIRM 157, 243, 268.

23. The priest must hold a host consecrated at that Mass when inviting the assembly to Communion at the *This is the Lamb of God* (S) 2002 GIRM 157, 243.

24. The priest must receive Communion from what he consecrated at that Mass (S) 2002 GIRM 85.

25. Extraordinary ministers of Communion approach the altar after the priest has received Communion and receive the vessels containing the eucharistic species from the priest (S) 2002 GIRM 162. (There is no prohibition, however, of such ministers coming into the sanctuary area earlier.)

26. Communicants should not pass the eucharistic elements from one to another (S) 2002 GIRM 160.

27. Communion under both kinds is permitted at the discretion of the diocesan bishop in addition to those instances mentioned in the liturgical books and to those individuals mentioned in the GIRM (O) 2002 GIRM 283.

28. The Precious Blood should be consumed at the altar after Communion. Excess consecrated hosts may be consumed or reserved in a tabernacle (S) 2002 GIRM 163.

The Order of Mass with the Participation of One Minister

1. The initial rites may take place at the chair rather than at the altar and the order of the actions and texts follows that in a Mass with a Congregation (C) 2002 GIRM 256.

2. The minister states the intentions of the general intercessions rather than the priest (as in 1975 GIRM 220) (C) 2002 GIRM 264.

Other Aspects

1. Priests may say three Masses on the Commemoration of All the Faithful Departed (All Souls) (S) 2002 GIRM 204d.

2. It is desirable to celebrate Mass facing the people whenever possible (S) 2002 GIRM 299.

3. An old altar no longer used for Mass should not be decorated (S) 2002 GIRM 303.

4. The tabernacle may be in the sanctuary, even on an old altar, but not on the altar at which Mass is being celebrated (O) 2002 GIRM 315.

5. Liturgical items and furnishings (ambo, chair, organ, tabernacle, vestments) should be blessed before use (S) 2002 GIRM 309, 310, 313, 314, 335.

6. The same priest must preside throughout the liturgy, except for the special case when the bishop is present who does not want to preside at the Liturgy of the Eucharist (S) 2002 GIRM 92, 108.

7. Texts for the prayer over the people are provided for each day of Lent (O) 2002 Roman Missal, Propers of the Season of Lent.

8. The Eucharistic Prayers for Masses of Reconciliation, although they have their own proper prefaces, may also be used with other penitential prefaces, e.g., the Prefaces for the Season of Lent (C) 2002 Roman Missal, appendix to the Order of Mass.

References

Abbott, Walter M., ed. *The Documents of Vatican II*. Trans. Joseph Gallagher. New York: Herder & Herder; Association Press, 1966.

Bugnini, Annibale. *The Reform of the Liturgy 1948–1975*. Collegeville: The Liturgical Press, 1990.

Built of Living Stones. Washington: United States Catholic Conference, 2000.

Cabié, Robert. *The Church at Prayer*. Vol. 2, *The Eucharist*. Collegeville: The Liturgical Press, 1986.

Flannery, Austin, ed. *Vatican Council II, More Postconciliar Documents*. Rev. ed. Northport, N.Y.: Costello Publishing, 1998.

_____. *Vatican Council II, The Conciliar and Postconciliar Documents*. Rev. ed. Northport, N.Y.: Costello Publishing, 1996.

General Instruction of the Roman Missal 2000. Study ed. Washington: United States Catholic Conference, 2000.

Huck, Gabe. *Sunday Mass Five Years from Now*. Chicago: Liturgy Training Publications, 2001.

Huels, John M. *Liturgical Law: An Introduction*. Washington: The Pastoral Press, 1987.

Hughes, Kathleen. *Saying Amen: A Mystagogy of the Sacraments*. Chicago: Liturgy Training Publications, 1999.

Institutio Generalis Missalis Romani (2002). Latin text available at:
http://www.usccb.org/liturgy/current/mr_001~1.pdf
http://www.usccb.org/liturgy/current/mr_008~1.pdf and
http://www.kkbids.episkopat.pl/wprowadzeniedoksiag/imgr/0.htm.
(This latter website, sponsored by the Polish Conference of Bishops, contains the text of the 2002 GIRM that shows the modifications introduced into the 2000 GIRM.)

International Commission on English in the Liturgy, "The Eucharist." Chap. 2 of *Documents on the Liturgy, 1963–1979—Conciliar, Papal, and Curial Texts.* Edited and translated by Thomas C. O'Brien. Collegeville: The Liturgical Press, 1982. (This chapter contains several relevant documents, including the 1975 General Instruction of the Roman Missal, along with earlier variants in the General Instruction.)

Jungmann, S.J., Joseph A. *The Mass of the Roman Rite: Its Origins and Development.* New York: Benzinger Bros., 1959.

Krisman, Ronald F. "Father (Always?) Knows Best: A Pastoral Interpretation of Liturgical Norms." *AIM: Liturgy Resources* 31, no. 4 (2002) 13–16.

Mahony, Cardinal Roger. *Gather Faithfully Together: Guide for Sunday Mass.* Chicago: Liturgy Training Publications, 1997.

Music in Catholic Worship. 2nd ed. Washington: Bishops' Committee on the Liturgy, National Conference of Catholic Bishops, 1983.

Norms for the Distribution and Reception of Holy Communion Under Both Kinds in the Dioceses of the United States of America. Washington: U.S. Conference of Catholic Bishops, 2001. Text available at: http://www.usccb.org/liturgy/current/norms.htm.

Palazzo, Eric. *A History of Liturgical Books from the Beginning to the Thirteenth Century.* Collegeville: The Liturgical Press, 1998.

Ratzinger, Cardinal Joseph. *The Spirit of the Liturgy.* San Francisco: Ignatius Press, 2000.

Smolarski, S.J., Dennis C. *How Not to Say Mass.* New York: Paulist Press, 1986. Revised edition, 2003.

_____. *Q&A: The Mass.* Chicago: Liturgy Training Publications, 2002.

Talley, Thomas J. *Worship: Reforming Tradition.* Washington: The Pastoral Press, 1990.

This Holy and Living Sacrifice. Washington: United States Catholic Conference, 1984.

Trautman, Bishop Donald, "Liturgical Renewal: Keeping the Virtue of Hope." *Origins* 32 (2002) 256–60.